My Gift
in Return

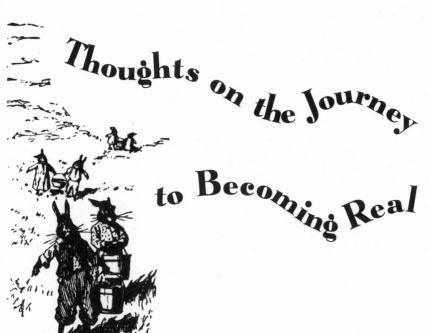

Thoughts on the Journey to Becoming Real

D. Barnes Boffey, Ed.D.

NEW VIEW PUBLICATIONS

CHAPEL HILL

ISBN 0-944337-44-9

Book design by Kelly Prelipp Lojk.

QUANTITY PURCHASES
Companies, schools, professional groups, clubs, and other organizations may qualify for special terms when ordering quantities of this title. For information, contact New View Publications, P.O. Box 3021, Chapel Hill, NC 27515, or call toll-free 1-800-441-3604.

Manufactured in the United States of America.

DEDICATION

This book is dedicated to
Heidi Dahlberg,
my wife.
You are my special gift.

and to
Jackson Thomas Boffey,
my grandson.
May you always live in the light of the Universe.

ACKNOWLEDGEMENTS

This book is the result of the energy and competence of many people. New View Publications owners, Perry and Fred Good, have always had a vision of creating books that really help people, and for years they have encouraged me to keep writing. They also introduced me to Kelly Lojk, my editor, who demands high quality, but does it in such a caring and respectful way that I almost enjoy the endless hours of editing that her comments require. She is a gift also!

I want to thank Kt Hoffmann and Heidi Hahighi for some important feedback on early drafts and also Linda Valley and Andy Williams whose enthusiasm and faith helped me through times of questioning and doubt.

As always, my wife Heidi Dahlberg gave me the support, honest feedback, and encouragement I needed to follow my dream; she never wavered in her request that I take the time and space to do whatever I needed to do to bring *My Gift in Return* to life.

Thank you!

CONTENTS

Introduction & Welcome xiv

Perspective 1

Focusing the Day ~ The Three Umpires ~ Expect the Best ~
Beauty ~ Wow, Save that Smile ~ A Healthy Madness ~ Don't Be
Fooled ~ Bum Diddley Oh ~ Make Metaphors ~ Turning on the
Light ~ Too Much ~ We Are Everything ~ We're All Just Parts ~
This Is It! ~ Maybe None of This Makes Sense ~ If It's Worth
Doing at All ~ Don't Be Afraid to Dream ~ Boredom Is a Lack of
Curiosity ~ How We Spend Our Energy

Yesterday & Today 25

Eating the Bear ~ Looking Back ~ Riding the Waves ~ New
Year's Day ~ Do What You Can Where You Are ~ One Day at a
Time ~ Life Is Not a Battle We Win ~ Focus on Your ISness ~
When Change ~ Wisdom and Pain ~ The Am of Became

Response-Ability & Choice 39

Good News, Bad News ~ A Question of Balance ~ Choosing
Emotions ~ Peanut Butter Sandwiches ~ Self-Esteem ~ Our
Special Places ~ Warm Impressions in the Chill of Winter ~
Creating Misery ~ The Cry of the Victim ~ The Power of
Helplessness ~ Losing Control Can Be Fun ~ What We Ask For,
What We Get ~ Making the Rules Harder ~ Practice the Future

Problems & Solutions 55

Perfection ~ Every Solution Has Its Problems ~ Problems We Can Be Proud Of ~ Which Side to Err On ~ Problem and Conditions ~ Sharpening the Ax ~ The Whimsy Factor ~ Three Zones and a Strategy ~ The Yes Zone ~ The Maybe Zone ~ The No Zone ~ Staying in the Yes ~ Allow for the Zigzag ~ Breaking Out of the Box ~ The Limits of Thinking ~ The Committee in Our Heads ~ Take the Next Step ~ Doing Nothing Isn't Doing Nothing

Spirituality 75

Believing in God ~ Spirituality and Psychology ~ Architectural Principles ~ A Thought ~ God Is the Architect ~ Understanding God ~ God Can Take It ~ And at That Point ~ God Laughs ~ God is Back ~ Love and Duration ~ In Tune with the Universe ~ Receiving the Universe ~ The Luckier I Get ~ I'm Just a Kid ~ Getting Right Size ~ Negotiating with God ~ Midwest Truck Stop, Heart of the Bible Belt, Put Your Hands on the Radio Blues ~ If You're Not Feeling Close ~ Two Things I Know ~ My Changing Relationship with God ~ Save Me ~ Help Me ~ Use Me ~ My Power Is ~ Being Misunderstood ~ Spirituality and Sexuality

Love 105

The Paradox of Love ~ I See Us Lying Mixed ~ The Search for Love ~ Softly, Pleasures of Our Being ~ Falling In Love ~ In Love, Of Love ~ Loving More Deeply ~ As I Contemplated Love ~ When to Stop Loving

Relationships 121

Seasons of Friendship ∼ With Some Friends ∼ Heart Clangs, Stomach Twists ∼ Going to Washington, D.C. ∼ Two Games of Tennis ∼ Who Cares? ∼ I Can't Accept the You ∼ Basic Assumptions ∼ Challenging Assumptions ∼ Clarify the Assumptions ∼ Hurtful Assumptions ∼ Assumptions I Accept ∼ Assumptions I Reject ∼ I Cried and Asked ∼ What You Promise ∼ Promising the Impossible ∼ Wedding Day: To Tim and Julia ∼ New Love, Old Baggage ∼ My Gifts to Our Relationship ∼ Obligation: The Cure For Generosity ∼ A Generous Spirit ∼ In All This Speed, Dear Lady ∼ The Relationship Killer ∼ Patterns of Conflict ∼ Winning by Default ∼ Wedding Day: A Reading ∼ A Kinder Disagreement ∼ The Thens and Therefores ∼ Awakening in the Mourning: a Reading ∼ A Function of Intimacy ∼ Expectations Hurt Celebrations ∼ The Rays of the Moon ∼ A Time to Leave ∼ A Better Set of Problems ∼ Double Jeopardy Relationships ∼ We Never End a Relationship

Anger 167

Facing the Anger ∼ Own the Anger ∼ Cherishing Our Powerlessness ∼ Not My Intention ∼ Behind the Anger ∼ Angry in the Right Amount ∼ When You Argue ∼ An Anger Freebie

Acceptance & Truth 177

The Process of Acceptance ∼ Step 1: Denial ∼ Step 2: Bargaining with God ∼ Step 3: Anger ∼ Step 4: Depression ∼ Step 5: Acceptance ∼ Sadness and Acceptance ∼ Stop in the Name of Love ∼ To Share Experience ∼ Knowing the Truth ∼ Personal Victories ∼ The Truth Still Scares Me ∼ A More Honest View of Yesterday ∼ A Hit on the Head ∼ An Accumulation of Lies ∼ Quality Demands Vigilance

Guilt & Forgiveness 195

Forgiving ~ This Day Was Called Christmas ~ Forgiving Ourselves ~ Forgive and Accept ~ Facing the Guilt ~ Changing the Standard ~ Decrease the Negative Judgement ~ Changing Our Behavior

Faith & Fear 205

A Knock at the Door ~ Asking for Help ~ Asking for Faith to Have Faith ~ Saying What We Want ~ When We Don't Like the Answer ~ Ready When You Are ~ July Morning ~ Messages from the Universe ~ Acting on Our Faith ~ Faith Misunderstood ~ I Thought It Was Happening ~ What You Gotta Do ~ Fear Begets Fear ~ Fear of Financial Insecurity ~ Where You Start Doesn't Matter ~ Kilometers Away

Masculinity 225

Defining Masculinity ~ What Boys Want to Know ~ Boys Are Boys ~ The Power of a Woman's Approval ~ Embracing the Beast ~ Fear of Touching ~ The Power of Safety ~ Sexualizing Everything ~ A Man Women Can Trust ~ Male Myth #142

Parenting 237

A Birth ~ Parental Vows ~ Each Day Upon Leaving ~ The Family Pictures ~ Waiting for Mom to Get It ~ Growing With Our Children ~ The Uneasy Lessons of Parenting ~ Roots and Wings ~ Character and Personality ~ The Important Stuff ~ The Fearful Truth about Drugs ~ What Drugs Do ~ When Drugs Stop Making Sense ~ Touching Moments ~ Family Vacations ~ More Yes, Less No ~ Emotions on Top of Emotions ~ "You're Weird" ~ More Than Consequences ~ Accepting Mistakes ~ The Dorm Room Conversation

Managing, Teaching, & Leading 259

Leaders People Follow ~ People Thrive on Trust ~ An Honest
Answer ~ Hurting Feeling, Hurting People ~ Resolving
Leadership Dilemmas ~ When We're Needed ~ They that Have
the Power ~ The Power to Forgive ~ More Than a Job ~ Thank
You, Mrs. Carol ~ In Service to Others ~ Working For, Working At
~ Shutting Out the Input ~ If You Don't Know ~ Surpassing
Expectations ~ Taking Time to Till the Mindsoil ~ The Safety
Curriculum ~ Information Freely Given ~ Roles and
Relationships ~ Carol's Song ~ Courageous Teaching ~ Fun and
Formality ~ Acknowledging the Spirit ~ The MVP

Maturing & Aging 285

Keeping the Child Alive ~ Life Stages ~ Growing Up and
Growing Older ~ Crying, Whining, and Complaining ~ Releasing
Volleyball ~ Changing Emotional Patterns ~ On the Road to 60
~ A Club I Want to Join ~ Stewardship ~ The Fire in a Man ~
Old Doesn't Mean Dull ~ Metal Fatigue ~ Death Is a Wake-Up
Call ~ A Final Goodbye to My Friend ~ When It's Time to Go ~
Thank You, Ruth ~ I Am Waiting for You

Thanks! 305

On Becoming Real

"What is REAL?" asked the Rabbit one day. Does it mean having things that buzz inside you and a stick-out handle?"

"Real isn't how you are made," said the Skin Horse. "It's a thing that happens to you... It doesn't happen all at once. You become. It takes a long time. That's why it doesn't often happen to people who break easily, or have sharp edges. Or have to be carefully kept. Generally by the time you are Real, most of your hair has been loved off, and your eyes

 drop out, and you get loose in the joints and very shabby. But these things don't matter at all, because once you are Real you can't be ugly, except to people who don't understand."

Margery Williams, THE VELVETEEN RABBIT, Doubleday Publishing, 1922

Real Is When

Real is not a flashy paint job or things that buzz
Real is what a man is now and not what he was
Real is when the world is suddenly on your side
A rainbow that comes to life in tears you've cried

    Toys who aren't Real last for only a day
    Mainsprings may break, they fade away
    Each child has the gift, no other can give
    To make you see, your reason to live

Real is when a child has loved you a long, long time
And even the games you play make a joyful rhyme
Real is when there's someone's heart that has room for
    you
A place to hide whenever your world falls through

Love is a whisper you hear in your dreams
How far away it can seem
But don't let your steps be slowed with despair
A day will dawn, when Real will be there

    Real is also very special, 'cause real is when
    You'll never have to feel again
    That you must be unreal again,
    Love can make you Real.

Barnes Boffey and Paul Pilcher, THE VELVETEEN RABBIT,
Dramatic Publishing Co., 1974.

Introduction & Welcome

Over the past few years, I have had an increasingly strong desire to honor those people who have helped me grow and develop as a person — in essence, those who have helped me to become more Real. *My Gift In Return* is my attempt to say thank you to those who have shared their friendship, honesty, love, and wisdom. From childhood to adulthood, I have been blessed with more than my fair share of "Skin Horses," caring people and wonderful role models. Some of these people have been friends for almost fifty years, others I have encountered for only hours or days. Each has enriched my life. The happiness and gratitude I feel today are due in large part to the many gifts I have been given.

Many of the writings that follow are extensions of concepts and thoughts that were passed along to me; I don't take credit for creating every idea. I can only take credit for writing them down and adding my own personal experience and knowledge to the process. As Carl Sagan said, "If we really wanted to make an apple pie from scratch, we'd have to start by inventing the universe."

Sometimes while writing I was struck with my inability to find the line between what I took as my own idea and that of someone else. There are thoughts in this book that are the result of conversations with others in which the give and take of information culminated in learnings that we both might legitimately think of as "our own." I have tried to give proper credit where it is due, and in situations where a specific idea has a connection with a specific person, I have tried to make that clear.

This book does not pretend to cover the entire spectrum of human behavior. I have written about what I know. I have many years of experience getting sober, working with boys, being a man, having relationships with women, managing employees, being a parent, being a friend, being a son, and experiencing the emotions of love, anger, hope, fear, guilt, and gratitude. I have also spoken of God in this book, and, clearly, I am only an expert on my own spiritual journey. It is with humility that I share my personal reflections in these areas; I hope they might help others as they live their lives.

The readings within are of two major types, what I call "Melody" and "Harmony." Melody pieces are prose and fairly straight-forward in their messages. Harmony pieces are mostly poetry and songs (with a few prose readings also included), and they represent a more lyrical way of expressing the Melodies in this book. Many Harmony writings were created earlier in my life. A few were written for weddings, some are tributes to people who have died, some are love poems, some are songs, and some are letters.

Where Camp Lanakila is mentioned, it refers to a boys' camp where over the past forty years I have been a camper, counselor, and director. I am only one of many dedicated people who have created this community where boys and men can become fine people. For me, Lanakila is a dream as well as a program and a place.

Another reference is to *The Velveteen Rabbit*. This is a musical adaptation of Margery William's wonderful book. I co-authored the musical with Paul Pilcher and Bob Love. My contribution was primarily lyrics and love, and some of those words are shared here.

This book is written to be read in whichever way suits you. Each reading is designed to stand alone (except when designated as part of specific series), but I also hope the readings grow in significance when read as part of a section or the whole book.

At the end of the book is a list of people who deserve my special thanks for the varied and significant roles they have played in my life. This book is *My Gift in Return* to them, although I am grateful beyond words for their generosity, friendship, wisdom, and love. They are my parents, children, elementary students, college students, campers, counselors, friends, lovers, teachers, colleagues, employees, clients, and mentors. I have also included some of my children's teachers, coaches, and mentors — as they helped my children, they also affected me.

I hope I have honored those who have helped me, not only with the ideas in this book, but by living the principles espoused within. As I wrote, I was reminded of the story of a boy who was drowning in the ocean when a passing adult came to his rescue and pulled him to shore. When they reached the beach, the boy said, "Thank you for saving my life. What can I do to repay you?" His rescuer simply said, "Just make it a life worth saving." I hope I have.

BARNES BOFFEY
June 2003

perspective

Focusing the Day

When a photographer takes a picture, she changes the camera's focus and depth of field to highlight different parts of any scene. She may chose to have the foreground in focus, or a single person, or to have everything slightly out of focus to provide an unusual mood.

Waking up each day and going to bed each night provide the same opportunity. The day is filled with infinite images and information, but we can focus our thinking and perceptions in order to create the effect we are after. If we want to feel grateful, we focus on what has gone well. If we want to feel needy, we focus on what we don't have. If we want to feel loving, we focus on those we care about and cherish.

I choose to feel grateful, peaceful, and spiritual so I begin and end each day with meditation, prayer, and readings. Each evening I write down a list of five things that I am grateful for that day. I've been doing this for over twenty-four years. In that time I have acknowledged over 43,805 things I have to be grateful for. Focusing becomes easier each day.

The Three Umpires

A world view is often best explained by parable or story. Here is one of my favorites. It concerns three baseball umpires discussing how they do their job.

"Well," says the first umpire, "it's really pretty easy. I go to the ballpark; I get behind the plate; the pitcher winds up and throws the ball. The ball passes the batter. There are balls and there are strikes, and I *calls 'em as they is*.

"Perhaps," chimes in the second umpire, "but I think it's not quite that easy. I go to the ballpark; I get behind the plate; the pitcher winds up and throws the ball. The ball passes the batter. There are balls, and there are strikes, and I *calls 'em as I sees 'em*."

"That's a beginning," says the third umpire, "but I think there's even more. Sure, I get behind the plate. The pitcher winds up and throws the ball, and the ball passes the batter. And we all know there are balls and there are strikes, but *they ain't nuthin' 'til I calls 'em*."

Expect the Best

For years I looked for the balance between being optimistic and being realistic. I wanted to have a positive outlook, but to do that I often felt that I had to deny the reality in front of me. A pessimistic outlook offered the benefit of protecting me from future disappointment, but I couldn't stand feeling negative and depressed.

I have found a balance I feel comfortable with: "Prepare for the worst and expect the best." I allow myself to imagine the worst that could reasonably happen, and then create a mental picture of my handling that situation. Then I am not so scared anymore, and I have also been *realistic*. With a backup plan in place, I can then put all my energy into expecting the best and enjoying the boundless creativity that seems to be alive and well in the universe.

Beauty

We were all taught that "Beauty is in the eye of the beholder." It may have been one of our first childhood experiences with the idea of relativity, and a step forward in understanding that there is no *right* answer to some questions.

It is also true that "Beauty is reality seen through the eyes of love." Beauty is the result of our perceiving with love. We actually create it when we love what we see. When I stop the loving, the beauty fades.

If we really took this idea seriously, we would understand that a beautiful day is not something we wait for, but something we create. And a beautiful life is not about the events and relationships we experience; it is about how much we can love and cherish those events and experiences.

"Beauty is reality seen through the eyes of love." That's beautiful!

Wow, Save that Smile!

Wow,
    Save that smile!

I don't know you.
    I never will,
But —
    I saw you smile —
    And that was enough

Right now.

Stop music, stop dancing, stop talking
    and then
    Can you smile?

I bet you can —
    because you're beautiful
    And that's enough

For me.

(1972)

A Healthy Madness

A nthony Quinn died yesterday. I will never forget his starring role in the film "Zorba the Greek." Zorba had one foot in the world of men and one foot in the world of spirit. When he danced on the beach, he transformed his simple life into an elegant existence.

He understood how to walk along the edge of rationality. He intuitively sensed the limits of thought and reason. He was able to connect with the passion and joy of dancing in the light of the universe.

At one point Zorba says to his staid English employer, "You think too much, that is your problem. Clever people and grocers, they weigh everything. A man needs a little madness or else he never dares to cut the rope and be free."

A healthy madness involves being crazy enough to fully enjoy the human journey, while at the same time being sane enough to realize how crazy we are.

Don't Be Fooled

Don't be fooled quite too easily,
   it wasn't really clay.
Creation's dose of navel lint
   has made us all this way.

(1972)

Bum Diddley Oh

Bum diddley oh hey hi ho hey hi ho hey
This is another quite wonderful day.
Sunshine is flooding the earth and — oh, boy
It lights up beauty for all to enjoy.
Hear chanticleer "cock-a-doodling" on,
Telling the nighttime it's time to be gone.
Forget your yesterdays, live what is now —
Isn't life wonderful, Golly, and How!
I can't express it so I've got to say
Bum diddley oh hey hi ho hey hi ho hey
Bum diddley oh hey hi ho hey.

Bum diddley oh hey hi ho hey hi ho hey
Life is an hors d'oeuvre, a chicken paté
Light up the candles let fireworks boom
Put on a smile and get rid of your gloom
You know it's easy to get out of whack
Count all your blessings not things that you lack
Ride on the carousel, let's take a spin
Start up the ferris wheel, let it begin
Each day's a carnival, that's why I say
Bum diddley oh hey hi ho hey hi ho hey
Bum diddley oh hey hi ho hey.

Bum diddley oh hey hi ho hey hi ho hey
Lead every hour in a joyous new way;
Don't take on life with a feeling of gloom —
Let it take wings, stand aside, give it room.
Throw out your arms and then fling out your chest,
Bust all the buttons on that tight old vest.
You'll just get ulcers if worry's your mate,
Follow your dream, and please don't break the date.
Give it a try and you'll find it will pay —
Bum diddley oh hey hi ho hey hi ho hey
Bum diddley oh hey hi ho hey.

Bum diddley oh hey hi oh hey hi ho hey.
English shout "Pip, Pip!" the Spanish "Olé!"
Hippies say "know your bag, do your own thing" —
Joy is the monarch, so "Long live the king!" —
Russians say "Tovarisch," "Vikings say "Skol!"
Irish say "Brrravo" with that Irish roll.
"Viva" or "Bene" or just "Down the hatch!"
If you're no linguist, then here is the catch,
All of the world will respond if you say,
"Bum diddley oh hey hi ho hey hi ho hey
Bum diddley oh hey hi ho hey!"

(This song was written in 1969 for the unpublished
musical "A Near Myth.")

Make Metaphors

M etaphors change perspective. Translating our intentions and behaviors into symbolic form allows us to draw power from the metaphor and perceive the significance of what we do through fresh eyes.

"If you could be an animal, what animal would you be?" Answering that question creates a powerful personal metaphor. When first asked that questions, I replied, "I'd like to be an eagle. They are detached and free and able to maintain a wide perspective. They are also strong and dignified."

Since that day, when difficult choices arise, I have been able to ask myself, "How would the eagle handle this? Would he be angry and scared, or would he face the situation with strength and vision?" Through the eyes of the eagle I want to be, I see the world differently.

Will our lives be blazing torches or smoldering campfires? Will we be trees standing firm in a heavy wind or leaves buffeted by the breeze? Do we want to be eagles or penguins or hummingbirds?

Turning on the Light

A quality life is not the result of *not* getting what we *don't* want. Quality comes from spending our energies on creating the positive, rather than eliminating the negative.

If we get too heavy, we need to put our energies into eating healthy foods, not *not* eating fats and sweets. If we are feeling guilty about a situation, we need to put our energies into staying centered and forgiving ourselves, rather than *not* feeling guiltily.

We don't push away the darkness, we turn on the light.

So many times we focus on what we have to stop rather than what we have to start. Just stopping the negative doesn't mean we know how to start the positive. The absence of ugliness is not necessarily beauty.

Too Much

Too much is
   not enough
      if the man
         is still crying

(1972)

We Are Everything

We can waste a lot of energy trying to figure out what we are and what we are not. Are we selfish or not? Are we racist or not? Are we weak or strong? Are we depressed or not? The problem is not with the answer; the problem is with the question.

In reality, we are all things. We are both depressed and not depressed. We are both weak and strong. We are both selfish and giving. We are both racist and not racist. Too often we try to push away pieces of ourselves in hopes of creating a stronger self-concept. Such a self-concept rests on a shaky foundation of misinformation. We need to embrace both our darkness and our light, our yin and our yang.

By acknowledging that we are both selfish and giving we resolve the question. Then we can move to a more important issue: "How does each of these traits show itself in my life and what am I doing about that?" We begin to create our answer rather than get stuck in the question. We choose a direction and make our choices, accepting that we will always be in transition and we'll never fully arrive.

We're All Just Parts

We're all just
   parts
   in this twirling,
   spinning
   ballet
   of existence

And the stage door
   is left open
      to enter
      to leave
      to stand

and in sitting
   you become
      the reason for all
      the spinning
         for it is all
spinning
   around
      you
         and
            you
and me__

I am the center of
my universe —
you are the center of
yours

And it's a joke:
a kick in the ass
and a pat on the back

To think you can do
what you
can't live with
and expect
to be happy

and there
my little flower

is the predicament we call today
the catastrophe we call yesterday
and —
the anxiety we call
tomorrow ...

(1972)

This Is It!

There's something about this story that I love. A friend of mine relayed it to me about his family travels as a boy:

My friend and his family — father, mother, sister — would be driving along in the car. At some seemingly random point, but always in a place with a nice view, the father would suddenly stop the car, everyone would get out, and he'd point to the landscape and say very simply, "This is it!"

Maybe None of This Makes Sense

```
maybe
    none
        of
            this
                makes
                    sense
                        to
                            you
                                but
                                    you
                                        to
                                            sense
                                                makes
                                                    this
                                                        of
                                                            none
                                                                maybe
```

(1972)

If It's Worth Doing at All

T ucked among all the little sayings that framed my childhood was this seemingly harmless adage, "If it's worth doing at all, it's worth doing well."

As life went on and I learned about perfection and arrogance, I was unable to reconcile this information with my sense of satisfaction in completing some tasks at a minimum standard so that I might go on to others I felt were more important. Filling in warranty cards for new products, spending time on meaningless paperwork, and a million other mundane activities cried out to be done quickly and with little thought.

One day, I heard the following words from an esteemed colleague: "You know, not everything worth doing is worth doing well."

Life's a little simpler now. I make better choices about how I use my time.

(Thanks to Faith Dunne.)

Strip Monday of the Blahs

Strip Monday of the blahs
   Tuesday of T.V.
   Wednesday of Prince Spaghetti
   Thursday of bowling
   Friday of beer
   Saturday of football
   and Sunday of God

and what of life is left?

   Man —
   bare-ass naked ...

(1972)

Don't Be Afraid to Dream

O ur dreams are like a fire at a campsite. We can go off and do other things, but in coming back to the fire, we return to the center, to the warmth, to the energy.

Sometimes we forget to dream. The daily barrage of reality takes up too much space in our heads. We begin to believe that this is all there is. Then a poem or a child or a friend or a random thought reminds us that keeping our dreams alive is what feeds the campfire. It nourishes our souls. Without dreams the fire dies.

Sometimes we are afraid to dream. We encounter so many disappointments that we become afraid of expecting too much. We try to protect ourselves from hurt and pain by letting go of hoping. We deaden our hearts so that we won't feel the hurt.

When we dream, we acknowledge the power of the universe. We return to the warmth and the hope. We rekindle the fire so it doesn't go out.

God respects me when I work, but he loves me when I dream.

Boredom Is a Lack of Curiosity

When we complain that something is boring, we are saying more about ourselves than we are about that thing. When we believe something is boring, we generally haven't taken the time to explore beyond surface level. Below the surface, everything eventually connects — and the universe is anything but boring.

Earthworms aren't boring. Taxes aren't boring. Bricklaying isn't boring. Basketball isn't boring. They all have a psychology, a history, a connection to greater issues of sociology and economy, and opportunities for profound insights by those who know and understand their significance.

Creatively connecting with people is also a matter of getting below the surface.

On the surface: What do you do for work? How many children do you have? ... Boring

And below the surface: When you were a kid, is this the kind of job you dreamed of doing? What's the hardest part of your job? What moment as a parent will you always cherish? Are your kids happier than you were at their age? ... Not so boring.

How to Spend Our Energy

Balancing the many emotional requests and demands of partners, children, friends, clients, and colleagues is one of the great challenges of being a caring person.

At some level we want to care deeply for everyone, but that becomes functionally impossible with the limitations of time, space, and energy. Giving to the point of self-destruction is not healthy. We need to make decisions about how to balance our own needs for love and freedom with our ability to maintain appropriate attention to the needs of others.

My friend Faith categorized the many people clambering for her attention into three distinct groups: intimates, family, and "caseload." Though somewhat tongue-in-cheek, these distinctions helped her understand her boundaries and priorities, and better focus her energy on intimates and family without draining herself with "caseload."

Part of being an adult is making choices about how we spend our energy and time in service to others — and learning to love ourselves well in the process.

(With thanks to Faith Dunne.)

yesterday
& today

Eating the Bear

Some days I think that the sum total of all I know after fifty-seven years of being alive is this: "Some days you eat the bear, and some days the bear eats you."

We have good days and bad days. We have successes and failures. "Some days you're the bug, and some days you're the windshield."

I used to think that if I just "did everything right," I could avoid the lows and be afforded only the highs. I was wrong.

It doesn't sound like much in the wisdom department, but just accepting that life is supposed to be full of highs *and* lows helps us weather the lows and enjoy the highs without fearing they may never come again. We get to do both: to eat the bear and get eaten by the bear.

Looking Back

How can we have our past play a reasonable role in our lives? Certainly some of our past is worth remembering, both the good and the bad, but we don't want to get stuck in the past. Focusing too much on the negative past can lead to feeling discouraged or guilty. Focusing too much on the positive past leads to complacency or yearning for the good old days.

"Look back, but don't stare," has worked well as a guideline for me. I hope it will work for you.

Riding the Waves

Life is a lot like surfing. The waves continue to roll in. Although success or failure may be determined by our ability to ride each of these waves, a great deal of our spiritual balance and well-being will be a function of our willingness to accept the eternal nature of the waves themselves and the relativity of the concepts of success and failure to our ever-changing awareness and standards.

Serenity, health, and wellness are not contained in the waves themselves. They are a function of our ability to face the waves, enjoy the rides, and accept the spills.

Letting go of judging ourselves as "good" or "bad" for our performance on any particular wave shows an understanding that responsibility doesn't necessarily imply blame. Sometimes a wave is simply beyond our level of ability. Sometimes we try something new and fail, even though it is an appropriate risk. Serenity comes with learning and accepting that how we ride is just how we ride. We could have done worse; we could have done better. Another wave is on its way.

New Year's Day

Wouldn't it be nice if New Year's Day really was a chance for a totally fresh start? Certainly we can make choices that will begin to take us in a new direction, but the reality is that we are all *works in progress*, the result of millions of choices that have brought us to this exact moment.

We don't instantaneously stop our lives and start again; there is the momentum of all that has come before. Our lives have inertia; we have created a great deal of energy headed in a specific direction. To make important and significant changes, we must learn to gradually steer in a new direction and accept that momentum is not immediately overcome.

Today, like any other day, we can make choices that bring us closer to becoming the people we want to be and the people God wants us to be. One step today doesn't seem like much, but by the end of the week we will actually be headed in a new direction — seven steps ahead of where we are today.

Do What You Can Where You Are

G handi said, "Almost everything you do will be insignificant, but it is very important that you do it." Every step we take is both a single step and part of a larger journey.

Life's path is not a predictable straight line. It is multi-dimensional, interactive, and spontaneous. If we believe that we can know with certainty the implications of any action we take, we are being egotistical and unrealistic.

One small step allows us to do what we can where we are. Though that step may not seem earth-shattering in the moment, every action, every thought, and every emotion we create has an effect.

Each step we take changes the world somewhat; we will never know how much until we act. Even then we may never know. It's an awesome responsibility.

One Day at a Time

The power of "one day at a time" was never clearer to me than during my seven-week hospital stay in the fall of 2000. The pain seemed endless; I had no mental or emotional protection from each day seeming like a forever that I couldn't cope with.

Living "one day at a time" was a way to narrow my focus and put energy into controlling what I could. "One day at a time" helped me refrain from taking on most of yesterday and all of tomorrow and feeling that I had to immediately solve all the issues that had arisen and might yet arise. "One day at a time" is a manageable slice of life. If we take care of this one, there is hope we can take care of the next.

There is also a paradoxical quality to stripping our lives of the worries of yesterday and today. Living "one day at a time" slows life down to a manageable pace, but it also turns out to be the fastest we can go.

Life Is Not a Battle We Win

Fear never disappears forever. We don't get rid of anger once and for all. We can't erase all our bad thoughts with good ones. We don't eradicate darkness when we turn on the light.

Character traits like fear and anger will always be a part of who we are, but as we grow and choose to act on different values, we move some to the foreground and others to the background.

Life is not a battle we win; there is no final victory over our darker side. Victory is a process, not an event. And part of that involves accepting that good will always come with bad, light with darkness, and the present with the past.

Focus on Your ISness

S ome pieces of our past are filled with wonderful memories, and some pieces of our past are not. It's hard to let go of the bad pieces if we keep repeating those patterns in the present. Too often we recreate the past in the present.

If we focus on being the people we want to be right now, we give ourselves the time we need to forgive ourselves for our past, prove to ourselves we don't have to repeat the past, and begin to see the past as *what happened*, not *what is continuing to happen now*. In short:

> *"Your wasness doesn't matter*
> *If your Isness really Am."*
> – Unknown

When Change

When change,
  the demand of
    becoming leading
      to be,
becomes a constant
    like time
    and space
  Then the reality we
    deal with,
    and as I say that,
    dealt with,
    catches us up in
  the spiral
    crescendo of our
        existence_____
and like a whirlpool —
  leaves us at the bottom
  of our soul —
that
  in relation
    leaves us stranded
      at the top of mankind —
  if there is a top —

Oh, Jack, let's not go parking tonight
Oh, Jack, let's not go parking
Oh, Jack, let's not go
Oh, Jack, let's not
Oh, Jack, let's
Oh, Jack,
Oh.

(1972)

Wisdom and Pain

Becoming wise is like boiling down maple sap to make syrup; we distill our painful experiences into drops of wisdom. If we have no sap, we get no syrup. Without painful experiences, wisdom eludes us. And, like the forty gallons of sap it takes to make one gallon of syrup, the more pain we have experienced, the more potential we have for wisdom.

Some sap makes better syrup than other sap, and the same is true of pain. Pain from facing the truth and making courageous decisions is a better source of wisdom than the pain derived by running from the truth and looking for an easy way out.

I used to regret that there had been so much pain in my earlier years. Now I see it as a gift; the wisdom is coming slowly. And even now, when times are really tough, at least I know I might get a gallon of syrup out of the deal.

The Am of Became

The am of "became"

   comes
      after "c"ing
       after "be"

       but before
        the end

        of "me"

         (19'72)

response-
ability
&choice

Good News, Bad News

The Good News: We are more in control of and responsible for our emotions and feelings than we even imagined possible. We are not merely victims of our circumstances, being bombarded by feelings and emotions we cannot control. We can take more responsibility and make decisions that will change our emotional and spiritual well-being. We can stop blaming others for how we feel and stop feeling sorry for ourselves because of the bad things that have happened to us. We are responsible.

The Bad News: We are more in control of and responsible for our emotions and feelings than we even imagined possible. We are not merely victims of our circumstances, being bombarded by feelings and emotions we cannot control. We can take more responsibility and make decisions that will change our emotional and spiritual well-being. We can stop blaming others for how we feel and stop feeling sorry for ourselves because of the bad things that have happened to us. We are responsible.

A Question of Balance

There are times in our lives when we are upset, angry, scared, and frustrated — when we feel out of balance emotionally and spiritually. When this happens, the following questions can help us gain balance again:

- How am I feeling?

- How do I want to be feeling?

- If I were serious about feeling that way, what would I be thinking?

- What are all my possible choices for a course of action?

- If I were thinking and feeling what I said I wanted to be thinking and feeling, which one of those choices would I make?

- If I make that choice, what's my next step?

We don't *feel* our way into a new way of thinking and acting. We *think* and *act* our way into a new way of feeling. This is often described as "Act as if." When we start *acting* and *thinking* as if we were *feeling* the way we wanted to be feeling, pretty soon we will be.

It sounds backwards, but it works. If you're not sure, just act as if you are!

Choosing Emotions

C an it be said that we *choose* our emotions? Do we really *choose* to be angry, sad, grateful, or depressed?

We don't specifically choose an emotion any more than one could say we *choose* heartburn. But, if we choose to eat hot peppers, the heartburn will likely accompany that choice. We can't eliminate the heartburn unless we change what we choose to eat.

Emotions accompany perceptions — and we do have a choice in how we perceive a situation or experience. As we choose a perception, we also choose an accompanying emotion.

A parent choosing to perceive their young child's behavior as disrespectful and rude will also likely feel angry or embarrassed. But asking that parent: "Are you choosing to feel angry and embarrassed?" would be met by: "Of course not! You don't think I *want* to be angry, do you?"

As we begin to look at things in a "different way," we also create different emotions. This can be liberating or depressing news; it all depends how you see it!

Peanut Butter Sandwiches

The burly construction worker opened his lunch pail on Monday and grumbled, "A peanut butter sandwich. I hate peanut butter sandwiches." On Tuesday, he again opened his lunch pail and scowled, "Damn, peanut butter again. I hate peanut butter sandwiches." Wednesday and Thursday brought the same situation.

On Friday, a co-worker who had heard, "I hate peanut butter sandwiches" for five consecutive days, finally couldn't take it anymore. "If you don't like peanut butter sandwiches," he asked, "why don't you ask your wife to pack you something else?"

"What do you mean, my wife?" answered the construction worker, "I pack my own lunch."

How many times do we encounter people who create difficult situations in their lives and then want sympathy for having to put up with the difficult situations they have created? How many times do we do it ourselves?

(Thanks to William Glasser for this story.)

Self-Esteem

Self-esteem is a belief we have about our worth and ability and value. My short definition would include the following thought as the centerpiece of that belief:

I am a good person who is capable enough to solve this problem, and I'll do the best I can. I'll make some mistakes, but I can handle this if I take my time ... I'm OK.

Self-esteem, however, is not something we *receive*; it is not something that someone gives us. We *create* self-esteem from the inside out. We build self-esteem through the act of *esteeming ourselves* for our behavior in the world. We look at how we handle situations, and we say, "I really respect myself for the way I dealt with that situation. I really like who I am when I act like this."

We can't build solid self-esteem before we act; it is through our actions that we build it. We can help others build self-esteem by challenging and supporting them as they take the time, build the strength, and find the courage to make choices for which they can respect themselves.

Our Special Places

We all have special places. As children, our special places might have been a hidden spot in the woods or at gramma's house. As adults, we may have a cabin by a lake, a summer camp where we have gone for many years, or a tavern where we meet with friends. When we go to our special places we feel balanced and whole.

It is not, however, the actual places that make us feel happy. It is *who we are when we are in those places* that creates our joy and peace and fulfillment. When we go to those places, we become people we really like. We treat ourselves and others well, and we match our vision of who we want to be. Our special places create an environment that provides conditions where we can thrive. In the end, it is not where we are, but *who we are when we are there* that makes a place special.

I don't really go to places that feel special; I bring my special feeling to the places I go.

Warm Impressions
in the Chill of Winter

Warm impressions in the chill of winter:
   my mind remembers bright green days of
      smile jumps and giggle runs

Balls of soccer-volley-foot and base fly past me as
   I visit the moment-places of summer that led me,
      sometimes willingly,
   through the tired times and lonely to the
circles of widening friendship,
   open fields of adventure,
      and shield fires of victory.

lake laps — evening taps — rabbit claps — high five slaps
Morey run — midday sun — marksman's gun — bracelets
spun:

Silly little moments sandwiched between Oreo cookie days
   of j-strokes, inspection scores,
      candy nights and tablesetting.

Goodness, badness, selfishness and joy;
   pain, love, energy, boredom;
      anger, tears and belly
         laughs.

The stuff of life in seven weeks of camp;
   the stuff of camp
   in forty-five weeks of life.

The pieces of ourselves that we found in each other
   were the gifts we gave ourselves
      as we opened our eyes with the sunrise
        and
      shut them with the dusk —

Reflections of love sparkle from the days of our being
together;
   I stand and stare at the dancing light until it becomes a
      breeze-gentled lake
        or a sun-kissed brook;
all these are wonders
   tucked in the pockets of my memory;

My gratitude deepens — I cherish my summer of visiting
   childhood;

I am deep heart thankful,
   dream touching softly and face smiling warmly;
      I swim in the thoughts of summer;
        Lanakila rests in my heart.
           How blessed I am to have you in my life.

(1993)

Creating Misery

If we want to feel miserable, the easiest way is to concentrate on the disparity between where we are in our lives and where we think we should be. As we focus on the ideas that we *should have more* and *should be more*, we increase our suffering at an amazing rate.

We can bemoan the fact that life is so hard and progress seems so slow, but expecting instant gratification on long-term goals simply fuels frustration.

Reversing this process starts with looking back at where we have been and feeling grateful for the progress we have made. Then we can find ways to refresh our perspective and to take a step forward. The following quote has always helped rekindle my faith when I lose perspective or forget what I have to be grateful for.

"When I really get discouraged, I go to the quarry and watch the stonecutter working on his piece of granite. And when the stone breaks open at the hundred-and-first blow, I know it was not that blow that did it, but all the hundred blows that had gone before."

– JACOB RIES

The Cry of the Victim

"I can't help it; it's just how I feel" is the cry of the victim. Victims claim that other people, places, and things cause their feelings and emotions. "I can't control my feelings; they just happen to me." The implication is that others will have to adjust because the victim can't change how he feels when others do what they do. "I am mad at you," cries the victim," If you want me to stop being mad, just stop doing what you are doing."

Pleading emotional helplessness is a wonderful way to claim no control over our emotions while at the same time attempting to exert tremendous control over everyone else's.

When we get tired of playing the victim, we may be ready to say to others: "I am angry right now. I am having trouble handling this situation. I want to feel differently, and I am going to work on doing that. It would be helpful to me if you stopped what you are doing, but in either case, I am going to work on getting back in balance."

The Power of Helplessness

The core belief of emotional victims is: "It's not my fault." Victims claim the world is causing their problems and that other people create their pain. They posit that there is nothing they can do to alter the unfair world in which they are powerless to change their feelings and circumstances.

There is power in being a victim. Victims get resources they might not get if they accepted responsibility. Others listen to them and provide a sympathetic ear, often validating the claim that victims are owed assistance due to their seemingly oppressive circumstances. They have leverage in relationships when others feel guilty about creating the victim's pain.

Relinquishing the power of helplessness is hard to do. If we accept responsibility for our choices, we may lose resources, sympathy, and leverage. The emotional price we pay for remaining a victim is high, but the price we imagine paying for accepting responsibility may seem higher.

Losing Control Can Be Fun

There's a wonderful line in a Pointer Sisters song: "I'm so excited, I just can't hide it. I'm about to lose control, and I think I like it."

It can be fun to be out of control, especially in ways that aren't harmful in the long run: breaking a routine, going with the flow, throwing caution to the wind, trying something new with no idea of how it will work out. These can be energizing experiences and testament to the fact that we trust ourselves.

Scary rides at a county fair, skiing as fast as the slope will allow, partying a little more than we normally would, bungi jumping, or seeing both the 7 and 9 o'clock movies consecutively can all feel like letting go.

Being a happy and successful human being takes a significant amount of discipline and vigilance, but it also involves the ability to really "let go" when the opportunity arises.

What We Ask For, What We Get

The down side of being a good sport is that you have to lose a game to show that you are one. Every attempt to increase the positive qualities in our lives necessitates a stressful learning experience in which those qualities can be demonstrated.

If we ask for patience, we will need to learn it in a situation where we are typically impatient. When we ask to be more forgiving, we are coincidentally requesting a situation in which we can rise above our anger and resentment. To face the fear of financial insecurity, we must experience financial uncertainty.

The universe tries to give us what we ask for, but the process is not always what we expect. There is no spiritual growth without spiritual challenge. There is no long-term growth without long-term effort.

Go ahead, ask!

Making the Rules Harder

If things are too easy, they aren't fun. Once we learn to master a task on a computer, or run a mile in a certain time, or consistently get fifteen things done in the time we had allotted for twelve, we want to try to do even more. Part of creating fun is pushing ourselves beyond our own boundaries and solving new challenges.

Someone once said, "Every game ever invented involves making the rules harder for the fun of it." Harder means more problems, more dilemmas, more decisions, and more choices.

When we stop challenging ourselves, we stop learning problem-solving skills. When we stop learning new skills, we stop having fun. The trick is finding a game or a job or a relationship that isn't too hard and isn't too easy.

Practice the Future

Our brains don't necessarily discriminate well between actions we imagine taking and actions we actually take. We can get a great deal of feedback on the emotional and spiritual impact of a potential action just by imagining taking it.

When we imagine confronting our boss, we experience many of the same feelings and emotions we would experience in actually doing it. Imagining our behavior is a way to test it out. We get a sneak preview of our feelings and emotions.

If we take the time, we can practice the future in our heads until we are comfortable with our next step. In working through a problem with a spouse, we can have fifty conversations in our head before we have the real one.

With enough time, we can practice the future until we sense a calmness that informs us that we have found a way to behave that allows us to be caring, strong, and safe.

yes maybe no

WRONG WAY

problems
&solutions

VIA RODE
N. RODEO DR

IGEBERG

?

Perfection

To live fully as a human being in the real world, we must consciously abandon the goal of perfection. *We are not supposed to be perfect.* Being human and being happy includes accepting and embracing our imperfection, getting beyond the disappointment of not being God.

Perfectionism is a way to drive ourselves and those around us crazy. It is egotistical in nature, and built on a foundation of fear. We believe that if we just try hard enough, we can do things perfectly and be perfect people. Not only is it impossible, it is not what God asks of us.

God asks that we enjoy our imperfection and love it as a reflection of our being spirit in flesh. To aspire to be perfect is to aspire to be God, but that job is already taken. The trick is not only to stop trying to be perfect, but also to stop wanting to be perfect.

Every Solution Has Its Problems

We spend our lives solving problems — big ones and little ones, complicated ones and simple ones. Too often we waste time and energy looking for the one right answer rather than accepting that every answer has both an up side and a down side.

If we allow our kids to choose what they want to eat, there are problems. If we tell them what to eat, there are problems. If we make time for ourselves in our busy work schedules, there are problems. If we don't take time, there are problems. It is important to remember that every problem has a solution, but also that every solution has a problem.

Imagine thousands of scales in our heads, each hoping to be in balance. Every solution we adopt will bring some of those scales into balance and others out of balance. There are no solutions that bring every scale into balance. The trick is to find solutions that bring the most scales into balance while accepting that perfection is not a human trait.

Problems We Can Be Proud of

A ccepting that every solution has a problem is freeing. We can then begin to embrace problems attendant with each decision, rather than naively hope to avoid them.

Once we accept this basic truth, we begin to face decisions differently. Rather than simply looking for solutions that have no problems, we learn to *choose the problems we are proud to have*. For example, if we trust kids, there are problems. They may perceive us as being gullible, they may lie, or they may not fulfill our expectations. But conversely, if we don't trust kids, there are problems. They may perceive that we are unfair, they may lie, they may not fulfill our expectations, and they may depend on others to monitor their behavior rather than taking that responsibility on themselves.

As we aspire to create homes and schools and camps where kids can thrive, the clear choice is that we must choose to trust kids. As we make that choice we also accept the problems that come with it. The choice confirms who we aspire to be, and we can be proud that the problems of trusting kids are ones we are willing to face.

Which Side to Err On

In situations where one choice seems as good as another, we can be stymied by how to make a decision. Suppose that as parents we can't decide whether we should let our generally trustworthy 15-year-old daughter participate in a co-ed parent-supervised sleepover at a boy's house. The arguments for "yes" may seem as convincing as the arguments for "no." How do we resolve the impasse?

To resolve this impasse, we need to have asked ourselves an even more basic question: "What do we do when we can't decide? If there is no clear decision, which side do we want to err on?"

Do we want to err on the side of trusting our daughter or not trusting our daughter? Do we want to err on the side of freedom or caution? Do we want to err on the side of trying to find a way to say yes or on the side of just saying no? We must decide who we want to be in order to decide what we want to do. Would you let her go or not?

Problems and Conditions

There is a big difference between problems we solve and conditions we live with. Whether to buy a new washing machine is a problem we can solve. How to get from here to Washington, DC, within a certain time is a problem we can solve. Whether to borrow money for a car or buy it outright is a problem we can solve. These are situations that can have finite and final resolutions.

The fact that our family members don't always act the way we want them to is a condition we live with. Aging is a condition we live with. Working to maintain healthy relationships with our children as they go through adolescence is a condition we live with. We never *solve* these issues, we simply deal with them in a process that is *always in transition.*

If we approach such conditions as if they are problems we can solve, we will be constantly frustrated. We will try to resolve the irresolvable and solve the unsolvable. A problem calls for a solution. *A condition we live with* calls for a next step, and then another next step, and then another next step ...

Sharpening the Ax

Abraham Lincoln said, "If I had five hours to cut down a tree, I'd spend four hours sharpening the ax."

He was a man who knew about planning.

The Whimsy Factor

Planning is a skill that leads to greater success in almost everything we do. Good planning means considering all the options, taking into account all possible variations, and guessing the effect of various major forces.

One component I have tended to overlook while planning is the Whimsy Factor, the presence of random and sometimes whimsical elements that seem to appear in every human endeavor. Reason and logic take us part of the way, but without including the Whimsy Factor, we are not being effective planners. The universe plays little jokes we can't predict, and as we leave room for those whimsical happenings, we become more in tune with a larger reality.

So next time you are planning a project and analyzing all the variables, make sure you leave room for the Whimsy Factor. You won't regret it.

Three Zones and a Strategy

(PART 1)

When a problem arises and we are confused about what to do, it is helpful to divide our options into three categories: steps that we know are possible for us right now, steps that we know we might be able to take, but not right now; and steps we know we can't or don't want to take right now. These can be called our Yes Zone, our Maybe Zone and our No Zone.

Suppose we are in a situation where our parents are visiting so frequently that it is causing problems. After considering the issue, we develop a list of possible next steps. We could confront them directly, have another relative contact them, see a counselor, avoid all contact, begin to lie about when we will be home, do some reading about this dilemma, think about moving, start a conversation with our parents even though we are not sure what to say, ask a sibling for help, write a letter outlining our concerns, or do nothing and hope the problem goes away.

Deciding which of these options fall within our Yes Zone, our Maybe Zone, and our No Zone will help us to feel less overwhelmed.

The Yes Zone

(PART 2)

O ur Yes Zone options are those steps we see as possible right now, even though they may not totally resolve the problem. Steps within the Yes Zone may be small, but would leave us ever so slightly better off than where we are currently. Sometimes these options seem insignificant in terms of solving the problem, but they are actions we could take rather than doing nothing. Often they are actions that help us change our perspective. Yes Zone options are well within our ability to do.

Regarding our parents' visits, Yes Zone options might involve seeing a counselor, reading about the situation, or doing nothing for a while longer. All are options we can imagine doing right now, even though they wouldn't solve the problem. They might make things slightly better and they wouldn't make things worse, especially if we are concerned about getting the rest of the family involved.

Yes Zone options provide a place to start and involve minimal complications.

The Maybe Zone

(PART 3)

In the Maybe Zone are actions we see as possible, but perhaps we are not yet sure if they will be wise or effective at this time. When we imagine taking these steps, we may feel queasy or perhaps we feel a sense of fear or dread. We can imagine taking these actions, but either the time doesn't seem right or we are unsure if they might not create more problems than they solve.

Regarding parents, choices that might fall into the Maybe Zone are: having another relative contact the parents, asking a sibling for help, or writing a letter to them outlining our concerns and desires. When the time is right, these may be reasonable next steps, but intuitively we know that now is not the right time.

Too often we are tempted to jump into taking actions in the Maybe Zone even though they don't yet feel right. This is a temptation best ignored. Waiting until the time is right will yield much greater results than plunging ahead. Before we enter the Maybe Zone, we are best served by taking steps in the Yes Zone.

The No Zone

(PART 4)

No Zone options are those we know we can't or don't want to take now. They are well beyond what we want to accept as reasonable choices. In this situation, No Zone options might include: Lying about our whereabouts, avoiding all contact, moving to another part of the country, or confronting our parents even though we are not sure what to say.

There is no reasonable doubt about options in the No Zone, just as there is no reasonable doubt about those in the Yes Zone.

As soon as we decide these are truly No Zone options, we can exclude them from current discussions and thinking. Spending energy entertaining No Zone options is most often a waste of time. When they arise, we should dismiss them quickly and focus our energy on Yes Zone and Maybe Zone choices.

Staying in the Yes

(PART 5)

In my experience, the most successful path when working through problems is to stay in the Yes Zone and let the small steps lead to bigger ones. Yes Zone steps provide experiences in which we can learn from the process. By taking Yes Zone steps, we gain unexpected insight and information, which then help us create new perspectives on the problem.

By staying in the Yes Zone, we allow the creative process to evolve. By doing what we can do, we learn enough to take on what we haven't yet been able to. We gain competence and insight. We begin to see and understand options we may not have seen before.

Staying in the Yes Zone acknowledges that the journey itself will teach us. Answers to difficult questions are rarely linear or one dimensional. Staying in the Yes allows us to be successful and provides both the time and safety to trust the process and let answers unfold.

Allow for the Zigzag

P roblems of any size or consequence are generally not solved solely with straight-ahead logical thinking. Creative solutions involve a twist of thinking, an intuitive leap, or an awareness of paradox that goes beyond the capacity of logic and provides a new perspective.

Albert Einstein told us that we cannot solve a problem at the same level of thinking on which the problem was created. Creative thinkers allow space and time for the zigs and zags, for serendipity, for the power of random thoughts, and for the freedom for their thinking to shift and wander.

If we keep sorting through a problem using the same thinking, we will stay stuck. It may be better to take a walk or bake a cake or take a nap or listen to an opera or talk to the flower lady at the supermarket or read a poem or practice yoga.

Answers, like everything else, work better when they are invited rather than forced.

Breaking Out of the Box

Much of life's confusion revolves around situations in which we are not sure what to do. The conflict between taking any one action can be very pronounced. What do we do?

One powerful tool is to decide who we want to be in the difficult situation and then do what that person would do. Searching for an answer outside the "doing" box allows us to see the problem for what it is: a creation of our own perception.

Asking ourselves who we want to "be" gives us the opportunity to see the problem from a different perspective. The essence of the problem then shifts, and previously hidden options may appear.

If I am torn as to whether to raise a specific issue with my wife, I can ask myself, "What would the husband I want to be do in this situation?" In reaffirming my desire to be loving, honest, and patient, the answer often becomes much clearer.

The Limits of Thinking

God must surely have a sense of humor. Why else would he give us the power to think? So many of the incidents in our lives that we now regret seemed like such a good idea at the time. So many of the ideas that made logical sense to us many years ago now seem like mindlessness.

Certainly thinking is a wonderful tool, but like any tool it is best used in some situations and not in others. Abraham Maslow said, "If the only tool you have is a hammer, you will treat every problem as if it were a nail."

Thinking allows us to traverse the universe of ideas, concepts, and thoughts. But to participate in the universe of the spirit, we need faith, intuition, and feeling. People who rely too much on logic and thought cripple their ability to see the unseeable, the most wonderful aspects of being human.

The Committee in Our Heads

What should I do next? We each have a committee in our head made up of different voices offering different suggestions to this question. "Do whatever feels good," cries one committee member." "Don't be stupid," warns another, "Just take the easy way this time."

Learning which committee members to listen to is a powerful tool in making decisions. The voices we listen to will determine the people we become. If we ask ourselves the question, "What am I going to do?" without addressing a specific member, we will find that the committee fights amongst itself.

Four committee members I have come to trust are: the courageous person I want to be, the honest person I want to be, the loving person I want to be, and the committee member who is interested in doing God's will as he sees it.

They have consistently given me good advice, but they often don't speak loudly enough over the din until they are asked.

Take the Next Step

If life is a journey, not a destination, then we are better served by focusing on our next step rather than the imagined end point. To answer the questions that arise as we travel, we need journey questions rather than destination questions.

Typical *destination questions* focus on a result. How can I solve this problem? What should I do to make things work out?

Typical *journey questions* focus on a process. What would be a good next step? If I were serious about being courageous, what choices would I be considering?

Destination questions push us to declare victory only upon arrival. Journey questions allow us to break down the process of living into manageable steps, each being an opportunity to acknowledge and appreciate success.

So, if you want to be more successful at asking questions that will help you acknowledge and appreciate success, what's your next step?

Doing Nothing Isn't Doing Nothing

S mart people often say, "Give me some time to think about that." Very smart people say it a lot. Allowing our brains the time they need to process difficult issues is part of making quality decisions.

When we feel up against the wall, the best alternative may be to take a nap — in other words, get out of your own way. We can allow our brain to work without a supervisor standing over its shoulder screaming, "Hurry up!"

Our brains don't stop working when we *do nothing*, just as we don't stop hearing things when we sleep. If we can eliminate our brain's having to tend to all the functions of our anxiety, it actually has more energy to focus on the issues involved.

Learning to do nothing in a stressful and confusing situation is an advanced problem solving skill. We do what we can, get out of the way, and allow our brains some quiet time alone to think.

spirituality

Believing in God

I have trouble when people ask me if I believe in God. I hear the question, but it doesn't make sense. To me it's the same as asking if I believe in love or honesty or hope or courage. Of course I do, but it is not really a matter of belief. I *know* they exist because I see them everyday. *Belief* implies they may or may not exist depending on whether I choose to acknowledge their existence.

I see courage every day, but I can't touch it or prove it. I see honesty every day, but I can't prove its existence scientifically. I see love every day, but I can't measure it with instruments. And I see God every day, but science doesn't have the tools to be able to measure God's existence.

So I guess the answer is: "No, I don't believe in God." To say I believe in God would understate what I absolutely know exists.

Spirituality and Psychology

The essence of spirituality is the search for awareness of God's presence and for knowledge of God's will. The urge for spiritual connection and oneness is often felt as an indefinable yearning or hunger. These urgings are spiritual in nature, but we experience them internally as urges to behave; we experience them psychologically. They become our psycho/spiritual instructions. Our best effort to follow these instructions involves our attempt to be as God would have us be, aligning our human will with our psycho/spiritual instructions.

Religion is filled with attempts to define God's will and our psycho/spiritual instructions. Some religious doctrines say we are instructed to be loving, honest, unselfish, and pure. Some psychologists focus on our instructions to be loving, powerful, playful, and free.

Whatever interpretation we accept, it seems clear that *the urge to be* is the manifestation of our spiritual essence, but the actions available to us as human beings are by nature psychological.

Although we may sense the music of the spheres in our souls, the only way we can bring it into being is using the instruments of head and heart.

Architectural Principles

P retending that we can design and live our lives without adherence to the laws of nature is pure folly. It is like expecting to build a house without accepting the laws of gravity.

There are also spiritual principles that define the essence and parameters of being human, and it is foolish to attempt to design our lives as if these didn't exist. These principles are not as finite as physical laws, but with training and attention, we can work with them as easily and deftly as we do with gravity and centrifugal force.

Spiritual principles show us that faith is stronger than fear, that we can use our intuition to know truth, and that spiritual guidance is available if we learn to listen in a special way. Spiritual principles help us realize that "we are not human beings going through a spiritual experience, but spiritual beings going through a human experience."

A Thought

When we meet,
   The God inside me
      strives with flowing determination
       to speak and rejoin with
         the God inside of you ...

Our egos resist the
   beauty of this meeting, and with
   faithless words and phrases,
   proceed doggedly
      to wrest
      ownership of this
      most precious of aspirations —
         love in ascendance ...

God knows our frailty, our need to possess:
   he gave them to us as options —
   a choice against which to measure
      our desires,
And, in his unending generosity, he also provided
   a yardstick called pain.

(1972)

God Is the Architect

There is an order to the universe and a path to spiritual fulfillment. Whether we choose to follow it or not is our choice, but without doubt, there is a *divine design*.

Our role is to try to understand that spiritual design and to recreate it in human form. God is the architect and we are the builders.

Understanding God

Many people spend a lot of time believing they can truly understand all the intricacies of the phenomenon we call *God.*

The simple truth is we are not meant to fully understand God. We have been given abilities to feel God, to see God's work in human events, to use God's power, and to communicate with God, but we are not designed to come to a final disposition on the nature of God.

As a friend of mine is fond of saying, "If God were small enough to be understood, he wouldn't be big enough to be God."

God Can Take It

A friend used to get mad at me when I would, as he described it, "use the Lord's name in vain." After hearing this three or four times, I finally said, "Peter, God can take it."

God doesn't care whether we describe God using a female or a male pronoun. God doesn't care whether we call him God, higher power, the oneness of the universe, the spirit of life, Allah, or Jehovah. If God were that concerned about the names he was called, he wouldn't be God. He'd be more like my second-grade teacher.

We all have the idea of God inside us, although we may express it in different ways. The important part is to share that idea, not argue about how we express it.

We may not all agree on what to call God, but we seem to agree pretty well on what it feels like when we are in the presence of God. Isn't that what God wants us to do?

And at That Point

And at that point a tremendous weight lifted from me. I knew that I no longer had any reason not to believe ... all the fears of letting go left me. They were useless, and I stood ready to understand.

My saying out loud "I believe in God" was not the beginning of years in a prison of dullness, it was not an acknowledgement of my own stupidity, and it was not the beginning of using faith as a crutch.

My heart opened. Or should I say, I opened my heart. And I could sense that all the indefinable forces in the world that I had always called coincidence, or luck, or energy, or nature, or love, or even cosmic balance were all simply reflections of the same light, like the sparkle of the facets of a diamond from a single sun beam.

What excited me was that I could call the diamond God without having to prove it to anyone or have it conform to anyone else's idea of a God.

Even then, it was not so much that I knew God existed, because in the secret parts of myself I had suspected that all along. It was that God could be for me the same as all the forces and powers I had known for so long. I no longer had to define what I understood as something different from God; God was all the things I already knew about — the mystery, balance, and energy in the world.

God was not a man with a long white beard; God was not a judgmental father I had learned to fear in Sunday School; God was not something or someone or somewhere that I didn't understand... God, in my life, was what I understood God to be.

And I knew that God was comfortable with that, and, by some "coincidence," so finally was I. My understanding of God in my own personal way was God's goal for me. We were both pushing in the same direction.

(This was written as a reading for a non-denominational camp chapel service in 1986.)

God Laughs

Every once in a while I can hear God laugh. Not a quiet demure little giggle that you'd hear at a dinner party, but a resounding belly laugh that fills the world and feels full of love.

I hear it most when my life begins to look like a scene from a slapstick movie. I may be running around trying to get 9,000 things done at once, and in my hurrying knock over a pile of papers that I had thought about moving five minutes before. Or I may postpone leaving for a meeting until the last minute, and then realize I'm out of gas. (Of course, I knew this the night before and could have filled the tank then.)

And sometimes there are "coincidences" that feel like a generous gift. When someone pulls in the driveway at exactly the moment I need help lifting a couch. Or when I can't imagine how I can make my day come together and then a client makes a last-minute cancellation and leaves me the opening I need.

At that point I generally look up at the heavens with awe and amazement, and that's when I hear the laugh.

God Is Back

I spent seven weeks in the hospital in the fall of 2000. I was in a lot of pain and during the first few weeks I was treated with significant amounts of morphine. As a recovering alcoholic, one might think I welcomed the chance to dabble in the drug high again, but all I remember is hating feeling out of control and having terrible hallucinations. One friend still jokes with me for telling him I was having flashbacks to Vietnam. (I had never been there.)

The hardest part of being on morphine was that the drug overrode my conscious contact with God. When I was doped up, I couldn't find God inside me. The drug didn't increase my spiritual connection, it lessened it. I relearned that a true connection with God feels better than any drug.

The day they took me off morphine, a friend asked me how I felt. It hadn't occurred to me before he asked, but even in my semidelirious state, my first words were, "God is back."

Love and Duration

S piritual love is timeless. When we are in the flow of the universe's energy, letting go of self, and relaxing into the flow of God's love, the limitations of time and space have no meaning. Our experience is both finite and infinite at the same time. We are totally empty and totally full in the same moment.

Some people sense this universal presence during childbirth, some through the intimacy of loving another, some on the edge of the Grand Canyon or the Pacific Ocean, and some through meditation.

Being of God's love is important merely in its existence, not in its duration. Too often we worry about "getting married before it's too late" or focusing on "how little time there is." If God's love is timeless, it won't matter how long we feel it. Finding that moment once may be enough for a lifetime.

As the Skin Horse says in *The Velveteen Rabbit*, "Once you are real, you can't be unreal; it lasts for always."

(Margery Williams, THE VELVETEEN RABBIT, Doubleday, 1922.)

In Tune with the Universe

When we align our human energy with the spiritual energy of the universe, we feel a profound resonance and transcendence from the cares and concerns of human form. We feel a timeless connection with the universal oneness, with the life force, with God.

Aligning ourselves primarily involves stripping away the things that stand between us and our awareness of the universal spirit: our fears, our busyness, our willful behavior, and our need for control. Like musicians tuning their instruments to match a particular note, we try to tune our lives to match the music of the spheres. When we achieve this, even for a moment, we know we are not alone. We know in an instant that a piece of the loving spirit of the universe is inside each of us.

Receiving the Universe

E very day we are bombarded by radio waves, satellite signals, microwaves, and electrical energy. But without a receiver of some kind, we would never know they were there. The arrogance of human beings is never more evident than when we stipulate that God may not exist simply because we haven't developed ourselves as good enough receivers to consistently hear the signal.

A trained submarine sonar operator can differentiate one submarine from another and "see" what is out there by hearing subtle tone changes in the recurring auditory blips. This is a highly technical skill that takes a lot of practice. What differentiates knowing from not knowing is the ability to listen and to interpret.

There is no question that there is a presence in the universe that can be called God. I don't take this on faith anymore than the sonar operator does with his evidence. The signals are there. It just takes training to hear them. Shhh. Listen!

The Luckier I Get

Filled with obvious disbelief, a golfing fan remarked to Arnold Palmer as he sank a sixty-foot putt, "Boy, are you lucky!" With an ease born of years of listening to such comments, Arnold Palmer quickly responded, "Yes," he said, "but I find that the more I practice, the luckier I get."

The same is true of spiritual well-being. If we attribute someone's serenity or ability to cope well to luck, we show disrespect to this person and to the power of the laws of being. Hearing from others that, "Spiritual growth seems easy for you, but I'm not that lucky," I often feel sad because I think they have missed the most important point.

The most important point is that each of us has access to spiritual growth. Serenity comes as a result of courageous and difficult choices. Serenity comes when we finally surrender to the laws of the universe and then practice, practice, practice.

I'm Just a Kid

I'm just a kid,
   I shouldn't tell adults

The when they know, the where they know
My correct length of hair they know

They know the how, they know the will
They know how many men they kill

Of time they know, of space they know
The colored peoples' place they know

They know what's kind, they know what's cruel
They know what I should learn in school

What's good they know, what's bad they know
What makes me sad and mad they know

Two questions stump them all — it's odd
They're: "What life means?" and "Who is God?"

I'm just a kid,
   I shouldn't tell adults

(1972)

Getting Right Size

In a recent TV sitcom, there was a moment when a female lead was sitting in the chapel of a hospital praying out loud. A friend who entered asked, "What are you doing?" The woman said, "I'm talking with God." The friend said, "You mean God, the supreme being, the almighty master, the maker of the universe?" The woman said, "Yes," and the friend said, "And you're doing the talking?"

It's hard to remember to stay *right size*. We can become too impressed with ourselves surprisingly quickly. When we start thinking we *are* God rather than reflections of God, we can spin out of balance at remarkable speed.

Stand on the top of a mountain, walk the beach, hold a small baby, listen to a person who has beaten cancer, watch the sun rise, hear a bird sing, or stand in the middle of a rainstorm. That helps us decide who should be talking and who should be listening.

I think I'll be quiet for a while.

Negotiating With God

At some point in my progression as an active alcoholic, it became obvious that my life was unmanageable. It could have been the car wrecks, the self-loathing, the loss of family and friends, or simply being broke. But somehow the information, "It's not working," finally got through the haze.

Recovery demanded that I allow God's wisdom and truth to play a larger role in my life, so I mentally negotiated with God to see who would guide the process. At first I felt quite magnanimous in giving God 10 percent and my retaining 90 percent, and since God didn't seem to mind, I lived with that for a while. As you might guess, I fared only moderately better, and soon had to renegotiate, begrudgingly moving to a 20/80 split.

Twenty-seven years later, God has about 87 percent and I have about 13 percent. But no matter how good things get, I fight the negotiations. And after all these years, God still smiles lovingly as he waits for me to find the courage and the faith to turn over the rest ... "OK, 88/12, but that's it!"

Midwest Truck Stop, Heart of the Bible Belt, Put Your Hands on the Radio Blues

Put your hands on the radio, and feel the Lord
Put your hands on the radio, and be healed
Put your hands on the radio, and hear the Lord
Put your hands on the radio, and be healed...

Sunday mornin' on the Midwest road,
Thinkin' 'bout my woman and my heavy load
Tryin' to find some tunes that will light my fire
Couldn't get much lower — gotta get much higher
(Sunday mornin' radio) (CHORUS)

My antenna's stickin' up I see,
Sort of like a lightnin' rod to G-O-D,
Every station's message is the same I find,
Put your faith in Jesus, he will blow your mind
(Station W-G-O-D) (CHORUS)

Reverend Mister Roscoe and Brother Ike,
Sending out the scripture on the D.J. mike
"Save your soul, son, repent, too,"
And all it's going to cost you is a buck or two
(Your dollars are tax-exempt) (CHORUS)

Turn off the radio, there's no good songs,
Just a lot of crap about my sinful wrongs,
Sittin' all alone with my spirit gone,
Thunderous voice above me says "Turn it back on."
(Father, Son & Holy Ghost) (CHORUS) & AMEN

(This song was written in a U-Haul truck with Brad King in 1974.)

If You're Not Feeling Close

We are born in the light of the universe, full of love and hope and goodness. This is our most natural and spiritual state, and we carry an awareness of this moment throughout our human journey.

Any time we get closer to that light we experience oneness, a conscious awareness of the spiritual essence toward which we are drawn for our whole lives. We may experience this desire as a yearning, a silent whisper, or a wish to return home. It will come and go, but it will never disappear.

These moments of awareness of both our spirit and our flesh define the edges of our humanity. And though our spiritual awareness may be lost or forgotten, in the deepest parts of ourselves there is a knowing that cannot be destroyed.

It is not the oneness of the universe that decreases; it is our connection to and awareness of it. If you are not feeling close to God, guess who moved?

Two Things I Know

There is a wonderful scene in the movie *Rudy* in which a veteran priest tries to help the confused and discouraged young Rudy make sense of his seemingly endless struggle to be a football player at Notre Dame. Rudy questions what God has in mind for him, and the priest says, "In all my years in the priesthood, there are only two things I know for sure. One is 'There is a God.' The second is, 'I'm not him.'"

It wasn't until I was well past thirty that I began to accept these truths, and even now I'm not always gracious about it. I didn't want to believe in God. I thought needing God somehow showed weakness and an inability to handle my problems by myself. I felt ashamed to believe in God. I thought I was supposed to do it alone. Wasn't that the measure of a man?

Coming to terms with our place in the cosmos is one of the central challenges of being human. What a huge relief to find we don't have to be the General Manager of the Universe.

My Changing Relationship with God

(PART 1)

Passing a quarter century of sobriety is a humbling experi-ence. Sure, it's great to know I have stayed away from a drink for all those years, but the true gift of my sobriety is an ever-deepening relationship with God.

My spiritual awakening has involved at least three major leaps in understanding. I think of these stages as "Save Me," "Help Me," and "Use Me." Generally I didn't fully understand the significance of each stage until I had already moved into the next one.

I don't know if there will be other major shifts in my sobriety, but God will reveal to me what I can understand, and I will do my best to put that into action when I understand it.

Save Me

(PART 2)

In my "Save Me" stage, all I wanted was for God to take the pain away and save me from the misery I felt at every turn. I was a drowning man, a total victim who cried to be rescued. I saw God as someone stronger than I who could manipulate the spiritual forces of the universe to save me. One version of my constant prayer was "Dear God, Please take this pain away and help me be OK. Please save me from the terrible life I have had and make things good for me."

My "Save Me" stage was really about survival — partly of my physical self, but more of my spiritual self. I just needed someone to rescue me.

Help Me

(PART 3)

The second major shift in my relationship with God was most easily defined by the overriding message," Help Me!" During these years I was genuinely interested in becoming a better person and trying to do God's will in my life. They were learning years, but I was very short on the information I needed to become the person I wanted to be. In my "Help Me" stage, I was asking God to give me the aid I needed to be a good person and to do his will. I was a student and a willing learner.

I knew God had the answers. Now I needed his assistance to help me understand them. My prayer through these years was, "Dear God, please help me do your will and help me be someone who is loving and honest and patient. Help me become a good person." I had evolved from mere survival and in this second stage I was focused on becoming someone I loved, liked, and respected.

Use Me

(PART 4)

"**U**se Me" marks the third stage of my spiritual growth. Here I find myself ready to ask God to "use me" in whatever way he sees fit to advance his spirit and way of being in the world. I am finally ready to do service without always worrying that I will not get enough for myself. I am able to feel the spirit of God in my life as well as a desire to share the overflow. I am ready to offer myself as God's servant to people calling "Save Me" and "Help Me."

My favorite prayer is the St. Francis Prayer, beginning each morning with "Lord, make me an instrument of thy peace!" I ask to be used and put to work! I ask to pay back what I have been so freely given. I ask to be a refection of God's goodness in the world in order to glorify God, not to glorify me.

My prayer today is, "Thank you, God, for all you have given me. May I use this strength and wisdom to share your love with others so that we might live in the glory of thy being."

My Power Is

My power is the truth
My goal is the light
My strength is in surrender
My trust is in God's will
My hope is in acceptance
My moment is now
And my way is sharing love
   in spite of fear
      in spite of pain
         in spite of doubt

(1993)

Being Misunderstood

No matter what we do, our well-intentioned behavior will occasionally be misunderstood by others, predominantly by those who have not yet reached the same level of emotional, spiritual, or intellectual development. The book *Twenty-Four Hours a Day* says it like this, "Your motives and aspirations can only be understood by those who have attained the same spiritual level as you have."

Misperceptions by those who have not yet traveled the road is unavoidable. As Abraham Maslow said, "You cannot perceive what you are not; it cannot communicate itself to you." Unless we know true kindness in ourselves, for example, we will not recognize it as kindness in the behavior of others. We may misinterpret what we see as self-serving, or pandering, or even an effort by the giver to get rid of his or her own guilt; but we won't recognize it as kindness.

And as we are misunderstood, so do we misunderstand others who have an even deeper understanding of their spiritual legacy. Or do we actually understand but just think that we don't? Time to grow a little more ...

(Twenty-Four Hours a Day, Hazelden, 1954.)

Spirituality and Sexuality

W hen we heighten our connection with the spiritual parts of ourselves, we also feel a heightening of our sexual energy. They are not different energies, they are different expressions of the same energy.

Sexual energy is a gift from God, a reflection of the spiritual energy of the universe. It is not something we should be ashamed of or ignore. Learning what to do when we feel it is not always easy, especially when we have learned to equate feeling sexual with always having to do something about it.

Once we understand the nature of these sexual feelings, we have more freedom. We can treat them as we would any spiritual awareness. We can act on them, cherish them, sit with them, ignore them, or just feel the power of the universe as it flows through our being. With time and faith, we eventually learn that there's nothing to be afraid of.

(Shakti Gawain also talks about this in REFLECTIONS IN THE LIGHT, New World Library, 1988.)

love

The Paradox of Love

In loving other people we experience the joy of doing God's will. The more I love you, the better it is for you, but also the better it is for me. Scott Peck says, "The paradox of love is that it is both selfish and unselfish."

When we understand our spiritual instruction to *be loving*, we can stop trying to pretend that loving others is only done for their benefit. Loving others is a beautifully selfish act; it is our path to finding spiritual fulfillment. If our loving helps another, we can feel both honored and grateful, but we love because we must if we are to find the God within.

We didn't create the laws of the universe. If we did, there would be no spirituality. God created the laws and we need to try to understand and live by them.

But when you think about it, isn't making love a selfish act a brilliant way to create a universe where people will love each other.

(Peck, Scott, THE ROAD LESS TRAVELED, Simon and Schuster, 1978)

I See Us Lying Mixed

I see us lying mixed in the ashes of each other,
    ashes gently stirred by the successive whirlwinds of an
       autumn breeze;
I see us, two in the passage of flesh, who through our
caressing
    of souls,
        find the center of the center itself,
          and ignite in each other's arms:
            becoming not in love,
            not of love,
            but becoming love itself ...

The image stirs uneasily in my mind ready for its
    birth into the world of doing,
        and I glimpse the power that we possess —

excitement beyond fear and
    fear beyond excitement;
        so much at stake —
Perhaps not the issue of life itself,
    but
        certainly the living of the life ... and I reach for you
and
        you are there ...

I'm deeper into me than I've ever been before —
my day-to-day has not demanded more:

until you loved me I could get by
    on what I and others accepted as exceptional,
        but now that's not enough.

My dreams have guided my reality at a distance appropriate,
but
    now as the
        courage born of caring drives reality ever closer to my
            dreams,
                I must find a new ideal ...
My vision of ultimate aloneness does not
    suffice the
        demands of the journey,

Today makes a mockery of the limits I impose on tomorrow,
    and the risk of allowing images of wonder,
        images of soultouch and enduring love
            craves to be taken ...
I want to "risk for a butterfly" – I do,
    and my excuses are falling away — for there you are,
        loving me,
            and my god speaks in my other ear;

but I'm worried that the time has arrived;
    you give me that kind of power,
and I'm not sure what that means ...

And I wonder if you'll have the patience to forgive my
    confusion,
        and I pray you will,

and as I write all the things I do,
   and think, and feel,

I realize again
   how much I love you.

(1991)

The Search for Love

The greatest value of an intimate relationship is the opportunity it provides for each person to *give* love. Before we understand that love is internal, we search primarily for others who will love us, hoping that their love will fill our emptiness.

In reality, it's not another person who creates the love we seek; it is the love inside of us flowing outward. The other person is the object of our affection, but it is the affection we send forth that feels so wonderful, so heavenly.

As the Beatles said so simply, "In the end, the love you take is equal to the love you make."

Softly, Pleasures of Our Being

Softly,
> pleasures of our being dance through my
> > awareness;
> miles divide us, but your head rests on my
> > shoulder,
> feeling safe and loved; we touch far from the fear
> > of aloneness.

My body misses yours — caresses, warmth, moisture,
flesh;
> > a yin without a yang, for
> there is a completeness about us which is a
> > treasure beyond words.

> Not completeness that leaves me crippled when
> > alone, but completeness
> > > that adds we to me and creates more
> > > > we-love in the universe.

That you understand my love for others is part of the
> foundation
> > of my devotion to you.
> > > You trust, you care, you love yourself and
> > > > you respect my being.
> > > I couldn't ask for more.

I pass between moments of loving intellect and heart
fire passion
when I think of you-me-us.
Part of me simply enjoys the idea of us and
part of me totally
enjoys the moment of we.

If I died today I would feel grateful for my time with
you,
and sure that I had experienced a joining that
reflected
God's love.

You move your head to kiss me, and I mine to kiss
you, and our eyes meet in
the kiss ... a testament to yes.

Sleep well, my love, gently, I am with you tonight.

(1997)

Falling in Love

F alling in love is fun! It's the magical experience of believing that everything will be wonderful. It's the belief that the person we are in love with is the answer to our prayers and that with that person, we may be able to perpetuate this feeling forever. It is the feeling of being one with the universe and the fantasy that because of this special person *happily ever after* may actually exist.

It feels so good, in fact, that we may want to fall in love on a regular basis. Not that we have to *do* anything when we enjoy that freedom; it's just fun to be swept away in the adventure of being in love.

Falling in love shouldn't be something that happens only once in a lifetime. Falling in love is an affirmation of the joy in the universe, and as long as we understand falling in love for what it is, we can allow it to happen more often without being scared that we will be a slave to our emotion.

Falling in love doesn't force us to do anything. It's fun if we can accept it simply for what it is, the emotion that accompanies boundless expectation and endless appreciation.

In Love, Of Love

B reaking the belief that love is external is difficult because of the words we use to describe our emotions. The time honored phrase "falling in love," often carries with it the assumption that we are "in love" because of what another person is doing; the belief that they are causing our feeling of "being in love."

Perhaps a more accurate way of describing the indefinable sensation of love would be to say that we are *of love*; that we are internally manifesting an extension of universal love. Being *of love* means reflecting spiritual goodness upon another, and as we do, becoming a part of God's endless loving energy.

In healthy relationships, people work at doing what they can to continue to be *of love*. They give what they want to get rather than worrying about falling out of love.

On Sunday

If you love me for loving,
     and not just loving you,
   then we can be one —

For I will fall in love again —
     with the man who eats spaghetti
   and slurps on his shirt

Or with a woman, for I have a
     constant love affair with all women;
   I am of them in the ultimate

I must treat all as one, for
   now I see that
     in the facts of reality we differ —
But in the essence of existence
We are as all is

If you must hold me to
   have me love you —
     then love is a joke
For
     love is a power all its own —
   and it must also have the
      choice to be ...

(1972)

115

Loving More Deeply

A tree continually blown by strong winds sends its roots farther into the ground. A muscle pushing against a heavy object grows stronger. Love that successfully faces adversity becomes deeper.

I used to be scared of having disagreements and difficulties in my intimate relationships. I prayed for smooth sailing and no problems; I was afraid that problems would chip away the love. It was all part of viewing love as something happening *to me* rather than *through me*. Once I understood that I had the power to create the love I needed, difficulties became opportunities to be a more deeply loving person.

That is not to imply that arguments, problems, and difficult issues are painless or quickly resolved. On the contrary, it is hard to be loving when I feel threatened or hurt or scared. In the hard times, that love is challenged and in meeting those challenges with those we love, we create the only real security we can hope for.

As I Contemplated Love

As I contemplated love,
   I remembered its simplicity,
   a gift I gave to you, and you to me, and God to us...

I forgot about the work demanded,
   the effort required to keep our new and
      growing love supplied and nourished;
For this flower needs the nourishment
      of honesty and truth
      and reality and faith —
all of which come only from the labors of integrity

But this morning, as I awoke amid a whirlwind of clashing
   wants,
   I remembered more.
Confusion enveloped me like a heavy mist,
      hanging between me and my soul
      and between my oneness with you ...
   it demanded immediate attention

"Not now, please; later when
   I'm better able to deal with it," ...
"Really, I'll take care of it soon, but not today," ...
   "Can't we just put this off for a while,"

But firm the truthforce stood,
      strength without malice;
      a tested friend demanding just due:
no fantasy, no illusion, no romantic vision ... work
no ecstasy, no peace, no you, no us ... work.

There is a time, my love, when in this struggle with
        doubt and death and yes,
    that I think I'm alone-
        that I'm all that understands about me.

I drop into a space alone with myself, clutching at
    visions of the peace and
        love I can become,
            and confront the power of the lie —

I look at the options in my humanity,
    and it's time, again,
to sample the eternities of heaven and hell,
    to release with doubting fingers my
        precious drop of eternity,
        and to struggle with stopping or going on ...

To exist is to do this work
To live is to do it elegantly

I wish you were here with me;
    though I fear it might make the choices
        seem easier,

        Something and everything about you promises me
    safety in taking you to this place —
        this core of me

where my fear is always that you'll laugh at me,
    my hope is always that you'll like me,
        and my dream is that you'll love me...

        even when you know it all.

                (1985)

When to Stop Loving

I'm not sure there is ever a good reason to stop loving someone. There are many good reasons to change the way we love others, but to stop all together seems self-destructive.

If God asks us to be loving and we stop, isn't that likely to cause us more pain than the struggle involved in continuing to love.

Learning to love an ex-husband or deceitful friend is very difficult, and that difficulty may be compounded by the fact that we don't even believe we should make the effort. After all, didn't they betray us?

Our love and compassion for an ex-wife or an abusive parent will need to take a new form and shape and character. We will need to find a way to care without leaving ourselves too vulnerable and a way to feel compassion that doesn't negate the truth. But finding a way to love others, even those we believe have hurt us, is the challenge God has set before us. When we cease the desire to love, our souls begin to shrivel. Loving is in our own best interest.

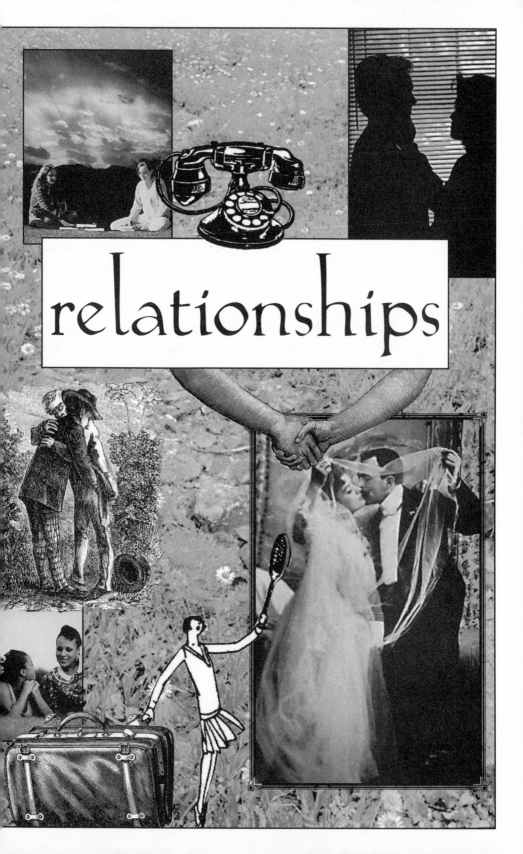

relationships

Seasons of Friendship

Long-term friendships are some of the sweetest there are. I have several friends I've known for more than forty years and with whom I still keep contact. Even when we don't contact each other much, just knowing they are in the world is a comfort.

There are seasons to friendships. The summer of activity, the fall of waning communication, the winter of little or no contact, and the spring of renewal. Friendships are never consistent in their intensity and form. As our lives change so does the form of friendships; that is part of the wonder of a true friend.

True friends do not demand a specific structure to the relationship. They are able to accept and enjoy the different seasons, knowing one will lead to another. They understand that the ebb and flow of friendship is part of its very nature, not something to be feared or fixed. True friends can be away from each other for years and when they get together pick up exactly where they left off. True friendship is timeless.

With Some Friends

With some friends, if I want to get together, I always have to be the one to call. With some friends, we may have one activity we do almost exclusively like going to the movies, but not much else. With some friends, I only hear from them when they are going through hard times. With some friends, we keep in touch daily or weekly, sharing the details of our lives. Good friendships do not need to fit into one specific format or style.

Friendships thrive when there is a minimum of criticism, when acceptance is high and judgment is low. We maintain friendships when we accept our friends the way they are. If we always have to be the one to call, so be it. If all we do is see movies together, can't we still have a great time together? When we need our friends to start being people they're not, friendships lose their vitality.

Friends accept you for who you are and don't need to change you for their convenience.

Heart Clangs,
Stomach Twists

Heart clangs — stomach twists — soul leaps
   Clarity in a moment of dazzling confusion,
      followed by the
         despair of
            finding what we have searched for all
            our lives
The spiral
   again and again
goes   con
   tinuously
around   around
   and dnuora and

until it stops for a moment to see itself,

   a spiritual dog with a human tail chasing itself to
     find something it
       will immediately let go upon catching.

Your pain is worth it and you are worth it.
   There is no surety except that you are moving in
     a dance that has existed since God told the
     universe the joke of mankind —
     the tempo is yours,
     the rhythm is yours,

but the dance is God's dance,
    and you are invited to do it.

There is nothing I can do but love you now,
    and send what I know to be healing thoughts;
       you are doing the rest.

You are supported by everyone who has had the
    courage to fly,
You are loved by everyone who has found healing in
    their center,

You are respected by all who know courage and
    fear for what they are.

Lie gently in my heart this night ... proceed with
your journey,
and applaud each step
       ... as you walk we all walk.

(1989)

Going to Washington, D.C.

I went to Washington, D.C., this spring to visit friends. I ran the concept of Washington, D.C., through the expectation file in my brain and it reported back: "Lincoln Memorial, cherry blossoms, Smithsonian ... lots of monuments." Cool, let's go!

I forgot that I was going to Washington, D.C., to be with my friends, and that these particular friends were pretty laid back, a little less driven than I am, and not as prone to pre-planning as I might be.

After several hours in D.C., I felt a little angry. We weren't going anywhere or seeing anything; we were just hanging out and talking. I wanted to be angry with my hosts for letting me down, but my problem was that I had never really consciously accepted the trip I was taking. Was I going to *Washington, my nation's capital,* or was I going to *Washington, the home of my friends?*

Once I understood the choice, it was easy. As it turned out, we only visited one-half of one museum; we got there too late to see the rest. But it was one of the best weekends I've had in a long time.

RELATIONSHIPS

Two Games of Tennis

There are two kinds of tennis games. One game is *relationship tennis* and the other game is *tennis tennis*. It's important to know which one we are playing or relationships suffer.

In *relationship tennis*, the relationship with our co-player is the primary reason for playing, and tennis is simply an activity that supports the friendship. I have a friend who is not especially good at tennis, and when she asks me to play tennis with her, *relationship tennis* is the game she is requesting. She doesn't say that specifically, so initially it was harder to figure that out. When I wasn't clear about that distinction, I used to go on to the court with the expectation of playing *tennis tennis*, an entirely different game. I often did well in the game, but not so well with the friendship.

In *tennis tennis*, the game comes first and the relationship is secondary. This is what we see in professional tennis, or when we play with highly competitive and skilled adversaries. I didn't used to think much about there being two games. I do now, and being clear which one I am playing makes tennis a lot more fun.

Who Cares?

For many years I dabbled in the assertion, "I don't care what anyone thinks." Caring about what others thought seemed to involve a subtle manipulation and loss of freedom, so the solution that kept bubbling to the surface was: "Don't give a damn about what anyone thinks; just do your own thing."

It sounded nice, in theory, but it never really worked, especially with people who really loved and cared about me. I knew intuitively that not caring what anyone thought was both foolish and self-destructive. I finally came upon an idea that seemed to resolve my dilemma: "I care about the opinions of people who care about me."

If someone knows me and values me, I am likely to take his or her viewpoint into account. If they are people who know nothing about me and want me to fit into a perception they have of who I am supposed to be, I care much less about their opinion. This doesn't seem like an earthshaking discovery, but it was a huge revelation for a young man who wavered between trying to make everyone happy and "damn the torpedoes, full steam ahead!"

I Can't Accept the You

I can't
deal with the
you that
accepts me
when
I can't
even
accept
myself _____

(1972)

Basic Assumptions

Every time we interact with another human being, there are basic assumptions that may be explicit or assumed.

When we talk with our children we may make a basic assumption that we should be listened to and obeyed. When we talk with our spouses, we may have a basic assumption that they will tell us what they really think. When we talk with our friends, we may have a basic assumption that they will support us in our point of view if we share with them an argument we had at work or at home.

These assumptions aren't necessarily accurate, reasonable, or agreed upon, but they are always present. Sometimes we are clever enough to question or evaluate these basic assumptions, and sometimes we get knee deep in pain before we figure out that we got started off on the wrong foot. Uncovering and evaluating our basic assumptions can prevent misunderstanding and pain.

I assume you agree.

Challenging Assumptions

When someone gets mad at me because they are frustrated by my behavior or choices, I am no longer willing to participate in any ensuing discussion based on what I consider to be a false assumption: that I am the cause of their upset. I am happy to be accountable for my behavior, but to also accept blame for the other person's reaction to my behavior seems to fly in the face of personal responsibility. If I am lucky enough to see the assumption before I am too deeply involved in defending, arguing, or rebutting, I can sometimes change the direction of the conversation.

For example, in my best moments, I might say, "I'm willing to discuss this situation based on the idea that you may want one thing and I may want another. I am not willing to continue based on the idea that because my wants are different from yours I have done something wrong. If you want to tell me how you are feeling and what I can do to help, I'm happy to talk. But I'm not going to start by having to dig myself out of a hole I don't think I belong in."

Clarify the Assumptions

During the early stages of my sobriety, my ex-wife and I still shared the same basic assumption: that I couldn't be trusted to be honest and forthright. Unfortunately during my active alcoholism that had proven true more often than I care to admit, and the basic assumption carried right into sobriety without ever being questioned. Not by her. Not by me.

Basic assumptions are rarely brought directly into focus, but as proof that it was there, our conversations would frequently end with questions from her such as, "Are you sure you're telling me the truth?" or statements from me such as, "I promise. I really mean it."

Getting sober is about getting honest, and I remember the day I realized that I had become a much more trustworthy person. I saw the assumption for what it was and no longer considered it valid. Hard to see, hard to change, but possible.

Hurtful Assumptions

As a child, a basic assumption in my family was that my brother was the smart one and that I was the big and physical one. Although I was occasionally perceived as quite clever, I was never regarded as an intellect.

On one occasion, my mother and brother went to see a Tennessee Williams play in New York City. Assuming I wouldn't like it because it was too deep, she urged me to see *A Funny Thing Happened on the Way to the Forum*, a musical full of slapstick antics, buxom women and not much intellectual content. It wasn't that Forum was a bad show or that I didn't like it. What hurt was the assumption that I wouldn't be able to handle the intellectual content of Tennessee Williams.

Twelve years later, when I received my Doctorate in Education, a friend sent me a card that said, "Congratulations on your graduation. See, you're not so stupid after all."

As I sat there, the tears rolled down my face.

Assumptions I Accept

It's not just other people who create the basic assumptions that are the foundations of our relationships. Each of us is an accomplice. As we grow older, we may be happy with the basic assumptions we have created, or we may find they are no longer useful. At this point here are some basic assumptions about my behavior that I willingly accept:

- I will go way beyond the norm in making an effort to work things out.

- I can be counted on to be a steadying force in most relationships.

- I am quite self-sufficient in most situations.

- I am someone who can be told the truth, even if it will be hard for me to hear.

- I won't lose my cool and say hurtful things when I get angry.

Assumptions I Reject

There are also basic assumptions I reject and will no longer help to perpetuate. Some are the work of others and some I created myself:

- I cause the pain of others. If they are mad at me, it is because I did something wrong.

- I am strong beyond all expectations. I will be able to handle every situation.

- When others evaluate my behavior, their evaluation is likely to be more accurate than my own. I am probably fooling myself.

- My sense of humor is weird or bad or gross or shameful. I'm too much of a "guy" in this area, and there's something wrong with that.

- I should conform to the expectations of others. People more powerful than I probably know best.

I Cried and Asked

I cried and
  asked
  Am I the type who should get married?
    and he answered,

You could use some security in your life ...

And Wednesday,
    while taking a shower,
      I laughed again.

(1972)

What You Promise

A good friend of mine had decided he was going to get married, and asked me for any ideas I thought might be helpful. I told him: "Be careful what you promise."

A promise is a guarantee that we will absolutely do what we say we will do. And yet we also learn as adults that life doesn't come with any guarantees. A promise of *never* or a promise of *always* is sheer mythology. Only God does *never* and *always*.

Successful people do different things at different times to adjust to different problems. It is very seductive to think we can promise to maintain the form of our relationship forever, that our marriage will always look a certain way. This is an effort to control what can't be controlled — the dynamics of the universe.

As the Danish proverb says, "Better deny early than promise long."

Promising the Impossible

O ne half of all marriages end. In my experience, one half of the remaining 50 percent are unfulfilling relationships that continue out of fear, obligation, and inertia.

The implication is not that people are bad. The primary problem in marriages comes from creating expectations that do not conform to reality. When people marry, they try to promise the impossible, only to learn after several years that neither they nor their spouse can keep those promises. Common *impossible* promises are:

- I will make you happy; you will make me happy.

- I will always do what I say I will do.

- You will continue to feel love because I love you.

- Love will protect us from the circumstances of life.

- We can guarantee our choices in the future.

- We can love each other unconditionally.

- I'll never hurt you or let you down.

When we express as promises those things that can only realistically be desires and intentions, we plant the seeds of failure and shame. We should only promise what we absolutely know we can do. That might also help shorten a lot of weddings.

Wedding Day: To Tim and Julia

Louder than a whisper
  More tangible than thought
  Love like eyes of yours touching heart so,
    soft in morning times of ripening wonder
     drew me open warmly
      toward faith found gift
       eternity.

I stepped cliff edge feeling forward
    past yearn horizon dreams of maybe
  finding step support next waiting
    never one had been before.

Risk takings, letting go, praying say it's certain
    in the cloudy land of doubt
  You were there mirror love ready willing
    finding simply strength in our growing
    hope of someday.

Glory moment songs of find you
    sang I almost unbelieving —
  You stayed accepting deep eyed promise
    holding ground where once fear settled
  In spite of me past lone surprising flowed
    I into we now love
     Can it — yes it — really be?

Our rhythm passion wisdom vow share
   Seedling love soft planted
      in the soil-friendships round us ...

Knows no limits, knows no ending, knows no dying.

Testament of love today in light —
   I give you my heart and touch me gently
   window see
      our souls distinct uniting ... now becoming we.

(Written for Tim and Julia Bucklin's wedding, August, 1995.)

New Love, Old Baggage

We often transfer the emotional baggage from an old relationship to a new one. If a former spouse used to return home angry and critical after visiting her mother, we are likely to get nervous when a new intimate wants to visit her mother. If a former boyfriend rarely followed through on promises, we may blow things out of proportion the first time a new partner doesn't move his shoes when he said he would.

Similar behaviors mean different things when done by different people. If the only time we heard "I love you" was when a favor was requested, we may feel less than enthusiastic when we hear those words anew, even if they are obligation-free.

In new relationships, we must be open to new interpretations and emotions, but first we must be aware of the old. When my wife and I first came together, these moments of awareness were often accompanied by the cry of "Baggage Alert!"

My Gifts to Our Relationship

My Willingness To Try To Work Things Out So That We Both Get What We Want And Need

My Willingness To Be Generous In The Sharing Of My Energy And Resources

My Desire To Be Honest And To Share With You The Truth As I See It

My Desire To Love You And To Pass Along To You The Grace, Love, And Forgiveness That God Has Given To Me

My Desire To Explore With You The Sensual And Sexual Aspect Of Our Lives

My Hope That You And I Will Share With Others A Way Of Being As A Couple That May Bring Greater Love And Peace To All We Meet

My Desire To Risk Sharing Myself At The Deepest Level, And To Maintain Faith That Our Relationship Can Thrive In That Honesty

My Willingness To Take Responsibility For My Own Emotions And The Desire To Lovingly Support You As You Grow In The Direction That You Believe God Wants You To Go

(On the day we celebrated our marriage, I committed to the above ideals in the presence of my wife, Heidi Dahlberg.)

Obligation: The Cure for Generosity

I enjoy giving gifts, especially gifts that involve time, thoughtfulness, spontaneity, and extra effort. When receiving these gifts, people often say, "Thanks, you didn't have to do that."

"I know," I sometimes reply with a grin, "if I had to, I probably wouldn't have." Nothing kills the joy of generosity as quickly as obligation. When we owe something to someone, it becomes a debt to be paid rather than a gift to be given. It becomes a *have to* rather than a *get to*.

When the basic foundations of a relationship are based on *owing* each other time, money, love, attention, sex, support, and togetherness, it diminishes the opportunities to give these as gifts.

It is fear, not faith, that drives the creation of obligations in relationships. We become afraid we will not get enough, and we create obligations to be sure we get our due. Even when a gift is given, it may be seen as just part of what is owed. Time and attention are deeper expressions of love when they are freely given and gratefully received.

A Generous Spirit

A nonymously giving to others is a powerful sign of spiritual strength. To give of ourselves and our resources without receiving credit gets to the core of true generosity — sharing without expectations.

It is a natural desire to give to others in order that we might be praised for our generosity, but to give solely as an expression of gratitude for what we have is a spiritual act. And difficult to do, for how subtle is even the need for God's acknowledgment — the hope that God knows what good people we are for what we have done. We want to get points for being so generous.

As I think back on my life, I must admit I have given relatively few truly anonymous gifts. There are a couple that come pretty close. But I must also admit that somewhere deep inside there is still a small part of me that hopes I will eventually be discovered and unmasked for my incredible generosity. Perhaps, if I'm lucky, that will never happen.

In All This Speed, Dear Lady

In all this speed, dear lady,
    there are moments that feel overwhelming and
        so very lonely;
And the illusion that no one else understands
    is not an illusion —
        no one does.
At times like this,
    I think what keeps me going
    is knowing that if I hold on, somewhere down the road I will
meet someone like you who,
    although you can't be there in my
        exact moment of fragility,
    understands and accepts my pain with
        intelligence, love, and a gentle touch.

You know my struggle because it is your own;
    and because your integrity is as precious to
        you as mine is to me, our moment of connection somehow
        compensates for the moment of pain and
        I am given the strength I need to risk again.

Something inside yearns for the continual stream of "thank yous"
    that we selfishly hope will follow all our acts of unselfishness,
        but the essence of our giving involves letting go of the need
            for praise on demand, and we are left in a bind that
            never gets resolved —
    it is with us each day as we awake.

The bind becomes holding onto the strength we get from giving
    and believing,
        while at the same time letting go of all of it so that
            we might enjoy it's fullness ...
No wonder there are moments where
    we need a lover's touch to give us strength;
when we feel like
    collapsing and saying "enough."

I can't be with you every moment to share your
    pain, and I know you
        wouldn't want that,
        but I can tell you that there are many, many
        moments when you are appreciated and loved when you
don't feel it directly.

There is always a safe place for you in my heart ... whether
    I say it or not ... please know you are loved.

And, since choosing "yes" in this world of "no's"
    and "maybe's" is
        always more courageous,

let's make sure we give ourselves the room we need to hurt, to
    doubt, to love, to heal,
        and to hope.

As you struggle with your choice to be,
    to you, with caring and respect
        I send my love.

(1986)

The Relationship Killer

Faulty beliefs and ideas destroy relationships as much as actions do. The belief with the highest relationship fatality rate goes as follows:

You make me happy by what you do for me and how you treat me. You make me unhappy by acting badly toward me, doing things that make me angry, and withholding from me what I ask for and need. I appreciate your love and kindness, but I need you to start acting that way more of the time so I can be happy in this relationship. You are letting me down. I expected more of you. And that makes me angry and disappointed. If you would just do the simple things I ask, everything would be fine. Then I would stop being upset with you.

Healthy relationships are created by those who create their own happiness, knowing that true security in a relationship is based on being able to be happy without needing to change the other person.

Patterns of Conflict

When too much time is spent trying to prove we are right, relationships suffer.

Healthy relationships are based on a win-win paradigm, working it out so that both people emerge from a conflict with their dignity, worth, and strength intact. Competition is fine when there is a choice to compete, but inappropriate competition can destroy a marriage or a family or a friendship.

If conversations are full of statements such as "No, you're wrong," or "That's not right," or "That doesn't make any sense," you can be sure the patterns of conflict are alive and well.

Living together should not be about winning or losing, it should be about living together.

Winning by Default

Too often, underlying the way we interact with others is a win/lose paradigm. We think in terms of competition rather than cooperation. We ask questions that search for a right and a wrong answer rather than searching for multiple right answers. We struggle in relationships to see who will control and who will be controlled, rather than aiming for co-leadership. We learn to perceive other people not as equals, but as less than or more than, good or bad.

Criticizing others is a way to win by default. It is a way to feel victorious without having to succeed. When we criticize others, we cast them in the role of losers, leaving the only other position, that of winner, for the taking. Criticism allows us to win without ever competing.

Regardless of the truth or our actual behavior, if we can paint everyone else as bad, it must mean that we are good. ... Or does it?

A Kinder Disagreement

So how can we have these disagreements and still keep relationships intact? Relationships flourish when both people feel valued and respected.

Most disagreements involve differences of opinion or differences of perception, not points of fact. Acknowledging this leads to kinder resolutions. Instead of saying, "No, you're wrong," you might try:

"That's not the way I remember it."

"I have a different way of seeing that than you do."

"I'm pretty sure it's true, but you may be right."

"It sounds like we disagree about what is going on."

A kinder form of disagreement takes nothing away from the validity of our own viewpoint, but also allows others to be valued. If it turns out we really are right after all, so much the better.

Wedding Day: A Reading

"I'm really glad we came," she said, as they moved toward the car in the parking area.

"Me too," he said.

As they walked, she shifted her hand toward his, hoping to find a soft squeeze and a loving touch. They needed to get back on track. It had been a rough week. His hand was there, but not the rest of him — but closer is better than faraway and at least they were talking.

"I guess it's good to come to your friends' weddings," he said. "It reminds you that marriage isn't easy. I hope they make it."

"I think they will," she said. "They've already been through some hard times, and they seem to really like each other."

"Yeah, but I'm not sure that liking is enough," he said. "I thought it was supposed to be about love."

"I think it is," she said, "but when you commit to live your life with somebody, I think love means lots of different things."

The talk slowed, but their thoughts kept moving. It's hard not to think about your own relationship at a wedding.

I remember the day I realized that being in love was not as important as being of love. I realized that love was inside of me, a gift I had already been freely given by God, a gift I could access by giving it to others. I'd waited so long for someone to give me the love I needed that I'd grown disillusioned in the waiting.

Finding love in hard times is made only more difficult when we look for it in the wrong places. When I look for it from you, or if I look for it in others, I don't find what I need. The love I really yearn for is inside of me, waiting only for my consent and commitment to leave me and find its way to others. When I allow love to pass through me, it becomes the most powerful force in my life.

Some say we love because it is the only true adventure. I say we do because it is our birthright and our path to transcendence.

When we can love another without demanding they deserve it, we have found the rhythm of the universe.

We are finally ready to join in loving union with another — ready to accept the challenge of loving each other as we each make choices the other may not like.

✳ *Love is friendship that has caught fire — it is quiet understanding, mutual confidence, sharing, and forgiving. It is loyalty through good and bad times. It settles for less than perfection and makes allowances for human weakness. Love is content with the present, it hopes for the future, and it doesn't brood over the past. It's the day-in and day-out chronicle of irritations, problems, compro-*

mises, small disappointments, big victories and working toward common goals. If you have love in your life, it can make up for a great many things you lack. If you don't have it, no matter what else there is, it's not enough. ✳

"I'm sorry about last night," he said. "I was wrong."

"Me, too," she said. "I shouldn't have been so judgmental."

Their hands tightened in thankful recognition of their forgiveness and they stopped for a moment to look at each other.

"I'm glad we go to a wedding every once in a while," she said. "I always remember why we married each other."

"Yeah," he said. "I guess it's as important for us as it is for them."

"I love you," she said.

"I love you, too," he said.

(Written for Tim and Julia Bucklin's wedding in August, 1995.)
✳ author is unknown. ✳

The Thens and Therefores

M aking decisions within relationships, no matter how simple, becomes complicated when we allow our minds to race ahead to imagined consequences. Within moments a relatively easy decision becomes monumental.

We create scenario after scenario, imagining all sorts of negative complications and problems arising, and then cripple ourselves even further by believing that our imaginings are real. (One definition of FEAR is False Expectations Appearing Real.) If left unexamined, "thens and therefores" can leave us powerless to take the first step.

For example: "If I tell my wife the truth about not wanting to go to the party, then she will be mad at me. If she gets mad, then she'll stay mad. Then we won't be able to work it out and that will lead to more fighting. Then we'll be upset all the time and eventually get a divorce. If we get a divorce, I'll be left all alone, and I can't handle being alone. I guess I won't tell her how I feel."

Or, if we want to face the fear, we can ask, "If I were the courageous and loving husband I want to be, what would I say to my wife right now?"

Awakening in the Mourning — A Reading

I haven't mentioned it much, but lately I've had mornings when I wake up early, before the alarm, and I just can't get back to sleep. It's usually at dawn, so there's enough light for me to see you lying next to me.

I am always amazed how peaceful you look; I can even see the face of the little kid you must have been. I see the face that your mom and dad must have seen when they looked in before heading to bed. Your breathing seems loud and somewhat irregular, and I am aware of it in a way I never am during the day. In the morning light, that faded scar above your eye and the tiny indentation on your nose seem more pronounced too. You lie there so unprotected, so vulnerable; I feel guilty for the questions that run through my mind.

"Wow," I think, "this is the person I married! Out of all the millions of people in the world, this is the one I said I'd spend my life with. How can anybody make a commitment like that and know it's totally right? What if it doesn't work out? What if I stop loving you? What if you stop loving me?"

I mean, there are things about our relationship that I have a right to be worried about. You get so angry sometimes, and you won't admit you made a mistake, and lately you don't seem very interested in my work, and I can't understand how you can spend so much money on clothes, and I wish you appreciated the extra time I take to do the cooking when you're out late, and you don't take much responsibility for keeping the yard clean and...

Whoa, what's happening? A minute ago I was thinking how peaceful you looked, and now it all seems so negative. If I have all these thoughts, does that mean it's not going to work? Maybe it's a sign that something is really wrong! Maybe we shouldn't even be together. I am afraid.

If you knew what I was thinking, you'd realize what a jerk I can be. After all, how can I claim I love you and still have these thoughts? How can I be married and still be so unsure sometimes?

I don't think I'd have the courage to share any of this with you if there also weren't miracles in the dawn. I don't know if God sees my confusion and reaches down to ease my struggling, but after all the questions something shifts and the answers start to come.

I know that beauty is reality seen through the eyes of love. I know that loving you is an ongoing choice I make and not a condition I should analyze like a stock market report. I know that my job is not to judge you, but to love you.

I know that faith in our relationship is not something that I should wait to get, but something I create on a daily basis. And I know that my fears of us not staying in love are really fears about my ability to maintain my commitment when I get disappointed or hurt.

I see God's challenge more clearly in those moments of the dawn. Our love really comes from the acceptance of each other's flaws and the decision to love in spite of them. Our happiness comes through our giving to each other, giving more than we think we have, more often than we think we should, with gratitude beyond what we can imagine, and by turning our fears about tomorrow over to God for safekeeping.

As the answers come, my heart feels full. In this instant I know how precious is our togetherness and how rich is our sharing. It all seems so loud in my head and yet you lie there quietly, your breathing steadier now, your eyelids closed peacefully. I can't just let the feeling pass, so I lean into your softness and stretch to kiss your lips. The kiss given, I pull back and gaze at your wonderful face. The confusion has passed: I know I love you!

And then, without even opening your eyes, like you've been with me all the time and known my every thought, you whisper the first words of morning, "I love you, too, sweetheart."

(This was written in June, 1998, for Simon and Karen Holdaway's wedding.)

A Function of Intimacy

After counseling couples for more than twenty years, I am convinced that the vast majority of sexual issues are really intimacy issues. If sex is a problem, the solution rarely lies in trying to figure out the mechanics of the sexual relationship.

If couples learn to talk and be close, if they reveal themselves honestly and safely to each other, an opportunity for increased intimacy and a closer connection with the spirit in each of them arises. As their spiritual selves are nurtured, so too is the sensual part of their relationship.

If they can keep these channels open, sex will likely become a natural extension of their connection. For the most part, the hardware is pretty simple; it's the software that causes the majority of problems.

Expectations Hurt Celebrations

My ex-wife and I were married for eighteen years. Were it not for the expectation that good marriages should last forever, we could celebrate that accomplishment with our friends and with each other. Instead, it is too often viewed as a failure and a defeat.

We can be proud that we made a home together and raised two wonderful children. We can be proud and thankful that we supported each other as much as we did, and we can be proud of the way that we operated as a family. We can celebrate that we worked things out to maintain a relationship for eighteen years, even with quite different personalities, and we can be proud that we still love and honor each other.

As a friend of mine says, "With anything else you do for twenty years they give you a gold watch and tell you what a hell of a good person you are. You stay married for twenty years and somehow it's a failure." Expectations hurt celebrations.

The Rays of the Moon

The rays of the moon gave us
    alternating moments of darkness and light,
illuminating our transition
    from caring about the light of the
      world we know
    to the light of the world we are.

I held your hand, and you mine, and we moved with loving
thoughts and feelings
    through the brambles of language,
      over the marshy patches of fear,
        and past the craggy cliffs of dishonesty,
      finally, to our heartspace,
        finding moments and minutes and timelessness

I awake again this day —
    you are forever a part of me —
      a part of me I love

I cherish our consequenceless being; precious tenderness
    that floats peacefully in my heart —
I celebrate our vulnerability and our courage;
    this loving changes my being

The moon is not in sight this morning, the
    sun has taken back the sky

But our touching beneath the crescent moon remains
    as a diamond in the dawn —

    a diamond with facets that sparkle in the revealing light
       of day-
            sparkling facets of trust,
                sparkling facets of truth,
                  sparkling facets of love.

(1991)

A Time to Leave

Finding the right time to leave a relationship can be confusing and painful, whether it is a marriage, a job, or a friendship. When possible, holding on until the time is really right can bring a sense of clarity that is not available if we leave too early, when we are still unsure of our motives, values, feelings, and emotions.

Leaving before we have worked through our confusion will likely lead to more hours of struggle after the departure. Forcing a difficult decision in order to avoid the pain of understanding is guaranteed to backfire.

When I am not sure if and when to leave a significant relationship, one very helpful choice has been to accept that *I would rather leave a year too late than a minute too early*. Waiting generally leads to clarity that isn't available when trying to hurry things along. When the time is right to leave, emotional dues are paid and the leaving, though difficult, is more a victory than a defeat.

A Better Set of Problems

It's hard to let go of the idea that someday we will find the ideal situation — that somewhere out there is a state of perpetual pleasure. Maybe it was all those fairy tales that ended with "and they lived happily ever after." A better ending might have been, "and they lived happily together most of the time, working out their problems and doing the best they could to cope with the challenges and problems of being human."

In whatever relationship we are in, there are issues and problems to be resolved. If we imagine that we might leave this relationship and find one with no issues or problems, well then "Welcome to Fantasy Island." In reality, we move from a relationship with one set of problems to a relationship with a different set of problems.

They may in fact be a better set of problems, or ones we respect ourselves more for having, or ones that are easier to handle, but there will still be issues and problems. And that is as it should be.

Double Jeopardy Relationships

When we stay in relationships that we know are unhealthy, there are two major issues. The first is the pain we go through in enduring present circumstances. In being unwilling to leave, we may endure continued sarcasm, lack of love or respect, diminishing self-esteem, or a loss of energy and hope. Unhealthy relationships take their toll.

The second issue is that while we remain in the unhealthy relationship, we are depriving ourselves of the opportunity to be in a healthy one. We are squandering time in which we might be loved or well treated or respected or proud. We deny ourselves pleasure by holding onto our pain.

Letting go of the present and opening up to an uncertain future can be frightening. We can never guarantee that we will find the healthy relationship we dream of. But by acting on fear we create more fear, and by staying in bad relationships, we guarantee that we won't find what we dream of.

And these are our lives; we are worth it!

We Never End a Relationship

We never end a relationship with a spouse, lover, friend, child, or parent; we only change its nature. Once we have become involved and connected, we can move closer or farther away, or care less or care more, but we can never totally disconnect.

We may not see these others physically, but moments will come when they pass through our minds and hearts. If we have not chosen to relate to them in a new way, simply remembering them may be as painful as seeing them face to face.

Once begun, relationships go on forever. When we surrender to this reality and learn to accept and alter our never-ending relationships, we take giant strides in creating happiness and freedom for ourselves and others.

anger

Facing the Anger

If we want to decrease the role of anger in our lives, we must first understand that anger is something we create, it is not an emotion that just happens to us.

And why do we create it? The process of living involves endless desires. We want all sorts of things: physical entities like computers or money, intangible things like winning a game or getting a new job, and abstract concepts like being treated fairly or world peace.

When we don't get what we want, we feel discomfort, the pain of unmet desire. We may feel it in our stomach or chest or head, and we realize that we are not getting what we want. We often choose anger as our best attempt to both express our pain and help achieve our desires. We choose it in hopes that the universe and other people will give us what we want.

Our anger proceeds from desires that are unmet, and we choose our own desires. If we choose them we can change them, and that is very good news.

Own the Anger

Wᵉ may choose to be angry when we don't know how to be powerful or gain control. When we blame other people and situations for making us angry, we give away even more power and control. When we are angry, our energy is best spent finding ways to be powerful without having to rely on changing those people or situations.

Being powerful may mean speaking up and saying what we want. Being powerful may mean setting limits on what we will and will not do. Being powerful may mean learning to sometimes say "no" when asked for help. Being powerful may mean refusing to take action until someone really listens to our point of view. None of these are easy, but without these skills we will likely keep being angry. When we act as powerful people in situations where we are unable to control other people or circumstances, we feel more in control of ourselves and less angry.

Cherishing Our Powerlessness

One of life's great lessons is that there are many things we cannot change — the greatest among them being other people. Often our first step in learning this lesson is to begrudgingly admit this powerlessness — all the time feeling angry and frustrated at our obvious lack of omnipotence. With time, we may move to a second step, a calmer acceptance, but this too is often accompanied by a simmering resentment. To be free of anger, we must move to accepting life on life's terms; we must learn to cherish our powerlessness.

When we cherish our powerlessness, we can energetically participate in relationships with full knowledge that we cannot control other people. Pretty soon, we stop wanting to. We learn to listen fully, to respect others' motive and desires, and to resolve difficulties. Thus, we may both win and walk away feeling whole. We learn to stop resenting the needs of others and start respecting their desires as being as valid as our own. Cherishing our powerlessness allows us to listen with a full ear and love with a full heart.

Not My Intention

A nger is normal, but not mandatory. Keeping in mind that we create our anger, we have more choices both before and after we are angry.

When we find ourselves being angry, one of the first things we can do is self-evaluate. "Do I want to be angry?" If the answer is *yes*, then we will most surely stay upset. If the answer is *no*, we can begin the gradual process of becoming calm.

Sometimes when I get frustrated or angry, my wife will ask, "Are you angry at me?" If I have taken the time to self-evaluate and decide that angry is not how I want to be feeling, I can say, "Yes, but that is not my intention. I want to let this go. If you give me some time to work on it, I'll be OK in a little bit."

Acknowledgment that I am angry is more honest than the denial of "No, I'm not!" The willingness to own my anger and the desire to let it go helps prevent the defensiveness that often leads next to, "Why are you mad at me? What did I do?" Of course, sometimes I still stay angry for a while. Oh, well!

Behind the Anger

S omewhere I learned that "behind anger there is always hurt or fear." Understanding this makes listening to angry people much easier. We don't have to get involved in the anger; we can listen instead for the hurt and fear, hoping to understand rather than defend and to assist rather than retaliate.

If we look at angry people as people who have been hurt, we can more readily decide to listen and to help them heal. If we think of angry people as people who are fearful, we can more readily decide to help them feel secure and safe.

Facing the anger of others is no longer a trial that must be endured; it is a situation in which we can be of service. And when we are angry, we need to remember to be of service to ourselves — to admit our hurt and listen for our fear.

Angry in the Right Amount

There is nothing *wrong* with getting angry. There is nothing *right* about getting angry, either. Its rightness or wrongness is not the issue.

Aristotle said, "Getting angry is easy. Getting angry for the right reasons, at the right person, at the right time, in the right amount, that's more difficult."

So many times we choose anger simply because it's quick and easy. It's actually a very effective behavior used at the right time, but if we use it too often, people stop listening and our credibility decreases.

When You Argue

If you're in an argument with someone and they get angry, you get something else, because angry is already taken.

(Thanks to Doug Walker for this idea.)

An Anger Freebie

Sometimes, when I'm alone in my car, I love to get really angry, ranting and raving over a simple mistake by a fellow driver who I can berate as stupid, moronic, and totally clueless.

Don't get me wrong, I don't open the window and yell at them. I just keep it in the car and build up resentment, which I use to justify swearing, yelling, blaming, criticizing, and feeling superior.

I call it an "anger freebie." It doesn't hurt anyone, and it gives me a chance to be angry in ways that aren't destructive. I see that as a healthy way to experience that part of myself in a safe environment. I get a chance to feel all that adrenaline rush through my veins. I remember the potential of my rage and am reminded that I do not want to be that way very often in the real world.

Sometimes I sincerely do get angry when I drive, but it's never as much fun as my anger freebies.

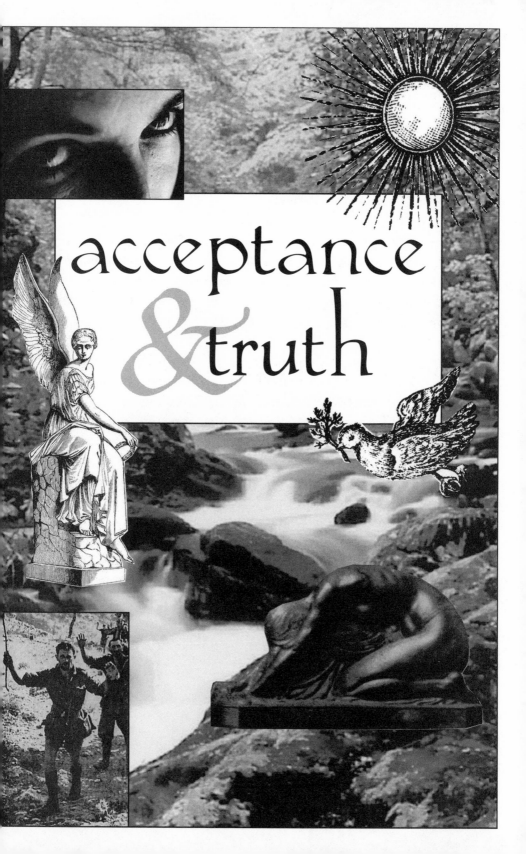

acceptance &truth

The Process of Acceptance

(PART 1)

The process of acceptance involves the "death" of certain expectations and fantasy. When we accept the reality of a situation, we may also be in a state of mourning for some of our hopes and desires. When we come to accept what is, we may also mourn for what is not.

We may have trouble accepting our growing older, or the reality of a divorce, or the fact that a body part may never work as well again, or the fact that we can't have children biologically, or the death of a parent, or anything else that threatens the quality of who we are and what we want.

Elizabeth Kubler-Ross describes five stages in the process of physical death and dying, and they hold true just as well for the death of desires, expectations, hopes, and dreams. Understanding the steps of denial, bargaining, anger, depression, and acceptance can help us move more smoothly through our resistance and fear, and enable us to embrace the bittersweet process of coming to terms with life as it really is.

(Elizabeth Kubler-Ross, ON DEATH AND DYING, Macmillan, 1991.)

Step One: Denial

(PART 2)

When we are faced with a reality that we do not want to accept, the first thing we are likely to do is simply deny that it exists.

"No, it's not true, my sister can't have cancer; she's the healthiest one in the family." "My son can't have a drug problem; we've been good parents." "I don't need an x-ray; there's nothing wrong with me." "I'm going to make this marriage work; the problems are not that serious and I don't believe in divorce." "I can stop drinking anytime I want; it's not a problem for me."

We hope that refusing to admit what's going on will save us from having to deal with it. The fear of what we might have to accept and our inability to know what to do if it's true are compelling reasons to try to shut the process down.

Denial works for a while, until the pressure of reality builds up and breaks through the barrier. But it does work for a while!

Step 2: Bargaining With God

(PART 3)

Denial may slow the process of acceptance. But as problems continue, sleepless nights grow longer, physical pain increases, and friends begin to make comments, we may reluctantly move beyond denial to admitting we have a problem. Still unwilling to accept the change that must come, we now put our efforts into finding a quick way to dispense with the truth we have finally and begrudgingly admitted.

This is when we bargain with God, asking him to take this reality away and replace it with something better. "Please God, don't make this be cancer. I promise I'll change my diet and stop smoking." "Please God, make my son not have to go into drug treatment. He can't have a problem. He's too young." "Please God, let us have children. It's not fair this should happen to us."

At this stage, we attempt to negotiate with the universe to keep our dreams, hopes, and desires intact. We believe that if we can just find the right prayer, God will answer and put everything back the way we need it to be.

Step 3: Anger

(PART 4)

"This isn't fair." "This is bullshit!" "My parents got divorced. I didn't ever want to have it happen to me." "God, you let me down."

Now comes the anger, the railing against the universe, the growing knowledge that we are powerless in the situations we want most to control. We hope our anger will be more powerful than the looming reality. Prayer didn't work, so now we hope that our anger will make it go away.

When we scream at a pregnant teenage daughter, our rage is not so much at her as at a universe that treats us so unfairly. We are screaming at the heavens: "It's not supposed to happen to me! This isn't fair."

Anger is our last stand, our final defense in the face of the oncoming truth. It is resentment toward God that we are not God's equal.

Step 4: Depression

(*PART 5*)

With the truth now clearly in evidence, we feel over-whelmed and confused. We need time to figure things out. We can't see the path ahead. We can't imagine living in a world that includes this reality.

We finally acknowledge that our sister does have cancer and there's nothing we can do about it; but we can't imagine living in a world where this is true. We know now that we can't have children biologically, but we have never prepared for this possibility. Our drinking has landed us in jail, but we can't imagine a life without drinking and the fun we believe we will miss without it.

We have spent so much time fighting the fact that our expectation or fantasy is dying that we haven't created options for what to do when the battle is lost. Our depression is a time of loneliness and self-searching. When we are in the middle of our depression, we feel like it will never end. It is time to search out our internal resources and to summon the strength to live in a new reality ... a reality we never wanted.

Step 5: Acceptance

(*PART 6*)

A nd then one day the sun breaks through the clouds. Acceptance begins when we can envision being OK in a world where our feared reality exists. We somewhat reluctantly begin to build new dreams and desires. We realize we can be the people we want to be even if the world serves up a dose of harsh reality.

Acceptance is well beyond simply admitting the truth. Acceptance is an acknowledgement that we can live with it, that there is a next step where we saw none before. We can adopt children. Drug treatment for our child may help him gain priceless insights. We begin to imagine ways to be good parents even though our teenage daughter is pregnant. We begin to build a future in which our mother has died, but where we can honor her in death.

We begin to build a world that includes the truth, and as we do, we feel more hopeful. As we move to acceptance, we put our energy into solving the problem, rather than fighting the problem. We surrender.

Sadness and Acceptance

W hen I am truly feeling sad — not depressed, but sad — that is a positive sign. Sadness is the emotion that accompanies acceptance, and being sad means I have accepted some truth that I had been fighting.

With acceptance of what is comes acceptance of what *isn't* — my old dreams and hopes and expectations. I feel sad as they pass on, but I cherish the sadness that tells me I have accepted that death. After all, they were just my ideas of how things should be; perhaps I grew too attached.

My mother died a few years ago. Now on Sunday afternoons when I would normally have phoned my mom, I feel sad. When I think back on my divorce and all that might have been, I feel sad. My sadness is my gift to myself, an acknowledgement that these things were and are of value. My sadness also shows me I am ready to move on, more hopeful than ever, because now I can learn to be happy with the world as it really is. My sadness tells me I'm free.

Stop in the Name of Love

Stop
   in
      the
         name
           of
              love
                what
                  you
                    have
                  not
                    started
                    in
                      the
                        name
                         of
                          love

                         so that you
                    may be at
              peace...

       (1972)

To Share Experience

When members of Twelve-Step programs speak at meetings, they are asked to share their "experience, strength, and hope."

They have found that honest and simple sharing of personal experiences can be amazingly helpful. Like Twelve-Step members, everyone benefits from sharing truthfully with each other: times we felt successful, times we endured failure, times we laughed, times we cried, times when we did God's will, and times when we did not.

As well as validating our ability to be genuine, an honest sharing of our experiences helps us realize that we are not alone. It helps us accept that we all have times of trouble and joy, failure and success.

It doesn't help to shade our stories so that we come out looking good. What helps is to speak from the heart and be real. What helps are authentic stories from which others can take what they need. What helps is sharing how we have moved beyond the shame of our past to an acceptance of ourselves in the present. What helps is the truth.

Knowing the Truth

Truth can have the effect of a babbling brook or a raging river. If we deny its energy, hoping to hold off the inevitable, the dam can only hold so long before it crumbles from the shear power of truth denied.

Truth comes to us gently at first, whispering to be heard. We sense its presence in our heart or stomach or chest. "Let me in," it whispers, "although you may not know it, I am sent here by God."

Too many times we greet the truth with fear. We deny it entrance and hope it will not come again. But it always comes back, each time more powerfully, until its request becomes a demand. And we feel it again in our heart and stomach and chest, each time less gently.

Learning that truth is more powerful than we are is an essential step in the spiritual journey. In the end, with God's grace, we learn that surrender is not defeat. Spiritual surrender is at the heart of spiritual victory.

Personal Victories

*"He that conquers himself is greater than
he who conquers a city."*
— Unknown

In trying to define the process of striving for internal personal victories for themselves and their campers, the Lanakila staff arrived at this definition of a "Lanakila Victory."

A Lanakila Victory is a "victory over yourself." It is a private achieving of a personal goal that you alone have decided will make you a better person. It is always something you are proud of having done, although it can and generally does begin with a small or menial task.

A Lanakila Victory may involve overcoming fear or self-doubt, but it is always an experience in which you learn to value yourself for what you have done and who you have been.

A Lanakila Victory is likely to be born of a desire to help other people, but it is always a matter of deliberate effort rather than luck. In achieving a Lanakila Victory, we learn who we are and who we can be, and we learn to listen to the still, small voice within us.

The Truth Still Scares Me

Physically recovering from alcoholism is hard, but it's nothing compared to the emotional journey, the hardest part of which is learning to tell the truth.

I still don't get it right all the time. I'm not sure I ever will. I have old habits where I shave the truth a little, mold it to be more pleasing to others, or deny it for a while so I can stall for time. In my alcoholic past, I believed that if people knew the truth about me, they wouldn't want me in their lives. Truth was an enemy to be feared and avoided.

I'm still amazed at how many times my first instinct is to lie. It's right there at the tip of my tongue. I have to be amazingly vigilant in assessing the truth or I can quickly slip back to old ways. I can still tell people little white lies so that they won't be as upset, or inflate a story to make me look more impressive.

I'm not that happy about it, but it's the truth.

A More Honest View of Yesterday

Over the years, my conception of what it means to be honest has shifted. As I grow more mindful and spiritually aware, I understand things I never understood before. I am called to a higher standard. What I had believed to be an acceptable level of honesty may no longer be acceptable.

During my divorce, I tried to honestly admit my responsibility for the process and to share that with my ex-wife. I wanted to complete the healing and move on once and for all. Not so easy! It turns out I wasn't done learning and understanding. As the years have passed, I have understood more about the process and my role in it. Doing so has meant many more conversations with my ex-wife.

It's not easy to be honest about a new awareness of the truth. Doing so means work, doing so means change, doing so means relearning what we thought we already knew. Doing so also means admitting that we may have been wrong.

We can never be sure of where a search for honesty will lead us. A desire for spiritual growth brings with it the never-ending challenge of looking at old situations in new ways.

A Hit on the Head

An old Yiddish expression tells us that "He who tells the truth gets hit on the head." Or as a friend once joked, "I know honesty is the best policy, but what's the second-best policy?"

When we commit to speaking the truth in relationships with others, we must also accept that it will not always be appreciated or understood. When we refuse to adjust the truth to fit the desires of others, we will not always get what we want. We may be accused of making things more difficult or not being team players or upsetting other people. The truth can be hard to accept, especially for those who may not have the courage to speak their own.

If we are looking for easy answers and relationships without upset, honesty isn't the best route.

Like anything else, the more we speak our truth, the better we get at doing it. We learn to face our fears of rejection and disapproval, and to enjoy feeling clean when the day is over. Speaking the truth creates problems, but compared to what?

An Accumulation of Lies

It's not the size of the lies that we tell so much as the fact that they accumulate. We can manage one little lie in the palm of our hand, perhaps even two or four or five or ten. But then we need a pouch to hold those ten while we put the eleventh in our hand again. As we progress we find we need two pouches, and then a sack to hold the pouches, and then a box to hold the sacks, and then a truck to carry the boxes.

Each tiny lie does not seem very significant by itself, but as they accumulate, they take up more space in our lives and are harder to keep straight. And the problem with lies is that we can't just take them to the dump, like garbage. The only lasting antidote is honesty.

When I came into recovery as an alcoholic, it took about six years to completely unload the barges I was dragging behind me. Little lies accumulated over thirty years take up a lot of space.

Quality Demands Vigilance

O nce we clean up the lies in our lives, we can begin to feel whole and beautiful. But maintaining this level of quality takes an ever-watchful eye, for even small incidents and issues can have a huge negative impact. One lie can have more power than we can imagine.

Picture the lobby of a lavish contemporary hotel; most are very impressive. The paintings, the waterfalls, the marble floors and the sleek steel architecture; the decorations are magnificent.

Now imagine a dog walking in and leaving a 6-ounce "greeting" in the middle of the lobby. The impact of that tiny dropping would be amazing. People would temporarily ignore the paintings, the marble would seemingly lose its luster, and the mahogany railings would somehow become invisible.

Until it was cleaned up, the dropping would command the attention of everyone present. And like that dropping, a lie in an otherwise honest relationship with ourselves or others can have a powerfully negative effect. The good news is that once its cleaned up, the beauty returns and may be even more appreciated than it was before.

guilt & forgiveness

Forgiving

Forgiving is an acknowledgement of the fragility of the human will, an acceptance of life and all its pain, misfortune, and randomness. Forgiving is choosing compassion rather than anger and hate, and accepting that the world is not as we might like it to be. Forgiveness is an act of spiritual surrender.

We have within us a spiritual instruction to honor and connect with the human spirit in others. When we are able to do that, we experience caring, compassion, love, and friendship. When we are unable to do that, we feel distance, anger, disgust, hate, and a sense of superiority.

Forgiving others is our reconnecting with the human spirit regardless of what has been done. Forgiving is the willingness to do God's will in spite of human frailty. To forgive is courageous; it is a sign of strength. To forgive is a compassionate choice. Forgiveness is a gift we give ourselves so that we can move from the darkness of an angry self to the light of a loving God.

This Day Was Called Christmas

This day was called Christmas
    And as we spoke of all that was ...
        we became Christmas, and could love again.

No peace can come between us until
    nothing comes between us ...

We must stand, each on his own,
    in the snow and son of life
To then feel
    the joy
        of finding and knowing our
            twogethernessence

And as it comes, the ripped shreds
    of mendacity lie strewn on
        the floor of the delivery room

And we are ...
    before we even know it ...

This day is called Sunday

(A poem written in 1972 to my brother, Dan, on the occasion of a significant beginning to our transition from brothers to friends.)

Forgiving Ourselves

If it is God's instruction that we love ourselves, to ignore that instruction is the height of arrogance and imagined self-importance.

"How can I forgive myself?" we assert, "What I did was so bad that I should never be forgiven."

Punishing ourselves is a non-spiritual effort to cleanse ourselves of spiritual pain. We occasionally do wrong things, there is no question of that. But God asks that we actively look for ways to love ourselves even when we have done wrong. Forgiving ourselves doesn't mean absolving ourselves of responsibility. In fact, it is just the opposite. Forgiving ourselves means using the energy we would have put into punishment to now focus on staying in concert with God's will. It means doing the best we can to make amends. We can't always make *things* right, but we can work to make *ourselves* right.

Forgive and Accept

Too often, forgiveness is perceived as the equivalent of "forgive and forget." We may think we are being asked to overlook what has gone on in the past, or worse, approve of it.

Forgiveness is neither forgetting or condoning. Forgiveness moves beyond the question of: "Is it OK that this happened?" to an acceptance that, right or wrong, "It happened." The goal is to forgive and *accept*. When we accept, we move beyond the incidents of the past to the issue of existing happily in the present as it is, not as we hoped it would be.

When we punish ourselves or others, it is our attempt to escape the need to forgive. It is a feeble effort to solve a spiritual problem with a human solution. When we forgive, we let go of our egos and search for the God in each other. Our ability to forgive may be our greatest gift and our greatest human opportunity.

Facing the Guilt

A t the heart of guilt is the word "should." We create guilt when we judgmentally compare ourselves to a standard of what we *should* have done or what we *should* be doing. Guilt involves making that judgement and then punishing others or ourselves for not measuring up.

Punishment involves inflicting emotional or physical pain to force conformity to rules or expectations. When we choose to feel guilt, we punish ourselves; as we try to create guilt in others, we seek to punish them.

When others attempt to "make us feel guilty," they are really seeking to punish in such a way that they are relieved of the burden of ownership for that punishment. They are off the hook; we are punishing ourselves.

Too often we hope to replace responsible action with feeling guilty. Responsibility means fixing what is wrong rather than humiliating ourselves for what we did.

Changing the Standard

G uilt always involves a negative judgement against a standard we believe we should have met. Sometimes that standard is reasonable, but often it is unrealistic.

As adults, we must rethink many of the standards imposed on us as children. But the question "Who gave me these standards and why can't I seem to change them?" leaves us stuck in the problem.

A more important task is to create new standards that fit with the adults we want to be. We move to a solution by asking, "If I were the adult I wanted to be, what standards would I be holding myself to?"

We begin a conversation with the adult in our head who can begin to imagine resolving this issue, not the child in our head who remains stuck. Breaking through old boundaries takes conscious effort and energy, but so does feeling guilty, albeit at a more unconscious level. Where best to place our energy seems to me a "no brainer!"

Decrease the Negative Judgement

The next step in changing a pattern of guilt is letting go of a negative judgement. This doesn't mean getting rid of standards, it means measuring ourselves less harshly. Three tools will help:

First we must accept that we always do the best we can with the information we have at the time.

Second, we need to ask ourselves, "Could we have done worse?" This helps bring to the fore the fact that although we made what we consider to be a bad choice, we deserve some credit for not making a worse one.

Finally, we need to learn to watch our behavior with compassionate detachment. "Isn't that interesting how I handled that situation? Hmmm."

(Tool No. 1 is an idea I learned from Dr. William Glasser. Tool No. 2 is a phrase often used by my colleague Diane Gossen.)

Changing Our Behavior

Once we develop reasonable standards for what we expect of ourselves as healthy adults, the next step in diminishing the role of guilt is to behave in concert with these standards.

One small example: I used to create a lot of guilt about being late. The standard I had adopted was that I should always get to places exactly on time or before. This became unworkable for two reasons. First, I didn't want to be run by a clock, and second, I found myself getting much too frantic about being even a minute late.

I decided that if I were the adult I wanted to be, I wouldn't worry about a few minutes. Then I adopted a personal standard that five minutes either way is still "on time." I respect my standard, and I like the kind of person who would have it. With my new standard, I am generally on time. When I am late, I remember that tardiness is not earth shattering. I apologize for my lateness, and I begin the task at hand.

Isn't that interesting how I handled that situation? Hmmmm!

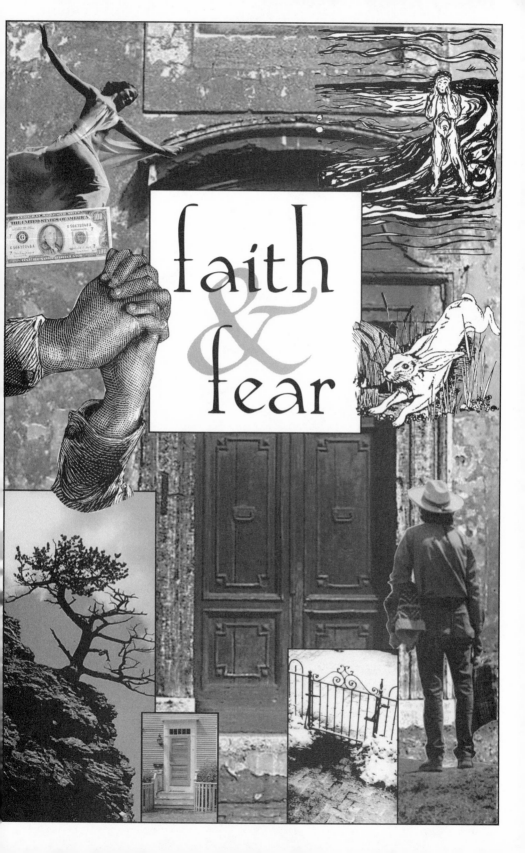

faith
&
fear

A Knock at the Door

Fear knocked at the door.
Faith answered.
No one was there.

(As seen on a greeting card, with no other information available.)

Asking for Help

Being human is not about total self-reliance. It was never meant to be that. But I keep forgetting.

When I feel trapped and scared — either because I don't see any choices or I'm afraid I can't succeed with the choices that exist — I am always amazed at my relief when I finally remember that I can ask God for help. Then I kneel and ask, and the help is always there.

It is a wonderful feeling to have the power of the universe to rely on. I am often stunned, however, that each time I remember to ask, it feels like a brand new revelation, something I'm discovering for the first time.

How could I forget such a gift!

Asking for Faith
to Have Faith

As an amazing demonstration of the generosity of the universe, it turns out that we can even ask for the faith to have faith.

If we don't have the strength to maintain our faith in God, we can ask God for that strength as well as for the faith.

What a truly generous idea. It would be like a bank lending you the money to be collateral on a loan they are going to give you based on that collateral. That's an idea only God could have.

Saying What We Want

We spend a lot of time imagining what we want, but too often it remains only at the level of thought. Thinking does help manifest our desires into being, but to use the power of the universe more effectively, we must express our wants externally, giving them definition and structure.

The universe aids us in getting what we want, especially if our wants are in accordance with the spiritual laws of truth, abundance, and love. In fact, when we work within these principles, we can learn to expect miracles.

Expressing our desires through speaking or writing helps us translate vague imaginings into specific words. Creating a picture or a song or a poem allows us to better define what we see and what we want.

I'll give it a try: I want what I write in this book to be a helpful gift. I want to be of love and service. I want to do God's will.

What do you want?

When We Don't Like the Answer

The best definition I have heard for prayer is simply "talking with God." In these interchanges, we often ask for things, some self-serving and some God-serving. One of my favorite stories involves an unwanted answer to a prayer.

A man hiking alone had slipped over a steep cliff and was hanging onto the cliff wall by a small branch. Sensing the branch loosening, the man looked up and cried to the heavens, "Oh, God, help me! Help! Is anyone up there?"

"Yes, my son," came the calm but awe-inspiring response, "I'm here!"

"Thank goodness," said the man. "I'm about to fall. What shall I do?"

"Let go of the branch," said the voice.

"What?" said the man, "Did you say to let go of the branch?"

"That's what I said. Let go of the branch"

Pausing for a moment to let the answer sink in, the man once again looked to the heavens and cried, "Is there anybody else up there?"

Ready When You Are

In all the times I have sincerely asked God for help, I have never been denied. I know that if I asked again today, I would not be denied, but sometimes I don't want to make that request. I can be very stubborn.

It's the simple things. I know I can't eat sugar on a regular basis because it sets up a physical craving in my body that I find very hard to resist. If I give into that craving, I gain weight, lots of it. Sometimes I'll be walking through the super market and I'll spot the ice cream. I know if I honestly ask for the help I need, "Please God help me resist this craving for sugar," the urge will go away.

I know what's good for me, but I don't always seem willing to ask for help. Sometimes I think I can still win the game alone. My permanent forgetter seems to be working full time. And so I eat the ice cream and set up the craving and gain the weight and realize again how powerless I am.

And God just smiles and says, "Ready when you are."

July Morning

Something dead is inside of me,
   the cracking trembling waves of
   pressurized fear rise in my chest and stomach,
and I wait,
   like a man having eaten bad fish,
     to throw up the poison so my body might
      return to harmony ...

But it is not the fish from the outside that poisons
   me ... it is years and moments of denying and
     running ...
   always being so sure that I couldn't face what
     I am facing now.

Your bodybeing with me tonight —
I am cradled against your breast praying that you love me ...
   and that we love each other enough to continue
     to do what we have done:
     losing our fears of each other and
     facing the fears of ourselves.

Your love and openness destroy any complacency I
   may have created.
Your warmth and love cry out for response;
   response that must be equal and clean,
   so the bonding will produce more love
   and openness

This death process is not one that proceeds or
    follows birth;
It is the same process as birth — they are not separate — they
are the inhalation and exhalation
    that comprise a full breath.

There is no moment in my life where I have both been so
scared and yet so full of love.

When I can, I will share with you a heart that is
    clean and pure- a love that
    expects nothing and asks for nothing except
       the chance to be received —
a truth so whole that its fullness transcends all fear and
worry and doubt.

Knowing that God is working inandthrough me
    and healing me, and us
       helps me know that this pain,
         seemingly disjointed from the center
           core of love
             is simply the labor that brings the
newness and goodness that I
    am and will be

There is movement in the heavens tonight;
We are in each other's souls.
    No one knows that but us ...
    we two are a multitude ...
    we two are a universe ... we too are love ...
looking through truth to find itself in the service of God

That you love me means so much to me...I am only beginning to know that ...
I pray I will follow without fear and proceed in this moment
with life ...
    alive in the truth,
        becoming of love,
            and faithfully aspiring to my divinity.

(1994)

Messages from the Universe

I know now when I start thinking of someone for seemingly no reason at all that, within a month or so, I will connect with that person in one form or another. I may get an e-mail, I may get a card or phone call, I may bump into them on the street or get a visit. But somehow well before I see them, I sense that we are moving toward each other.

When I am trying to figure out a problem, I see billboards that give me answers. I stumble across poems or notes that say exactly what I need. Or I hear a line in a TV show that seems like a direct answer to my question.

Some would say that I see what I need to see, that the information is always there. Perhaps, but I know that when I am patient and attentive, I get what my friend Perry calls *messages from the universe* in all sorts of interesting and diverse ways. There seems to be a universal energy that wants to help me stay in balance. I don't understand it, but it sure is fun to see where the next message will come from.

(With thanks to Perry Good.)

Acting on Our Faith

A cting on faith is the antidote to fear. Acting on faith allows us to access the essential goodness of the universe. Acting on faith is believing that our lives will be more effective and successful if we open ourselves to the spiritual as well as the logical. Acting on faith is an affirmation of the belief that problems can be solved in more creative ways than we might ever imagine. Acting on faith is trusting that we are not alone.

Questions that help us create faithful actions:

- "If I had faith in the goodness and creativity of the universe, what would be my next step?"

- "If I were to act out of faith instead of fear, what would be my next step?"

- "If I were doing God's will in this situation, what would be my next step?"

And as we take these steps, we learn to have faith in our faith.

Faith Misunderstood

A man was in the path of a flooding river, and the water had risen to his front door. A neighbor came by in a boat and asked him if he wanted a ride to safety. "No thanks," said the man, "God is going to save me."

A few hours later the torrential water had risen to the second floor. Another boat came by, and the man was offered assistance again. "No thank you," he affirmed, "God is going to save me."

Finally the water had risen so high that the man was on his roof and the waters were still rising. A helicopter paused overhead and the pilot shouted, "I'll send down a rope." "No thanks," said the man resolutely, "God is going to save me."

Well, he drowned. And as he was speaking to God that night he posed the obvious question: "Lord," he said, "I had faith in you and you let me down."

"I don't know what else I could have done," God said, "I sent you two boats and a helicopter."

I Thought It Was Happening

A trickle of hope has crept into my heart
The dreams of tomorrow tear this day apart
This magic I yearn for is love's ecstasy
I thought it was happening,
Thought it was happening, thought it was happening to me

Tearing down walls built of tears I have cried
That something quite lovely would take root inside
A blossom within me, a beautiful tree
I thought it was happening,
Thought it was happening, thought it was happening to me

The wisdom of age passes on to its youth
In words very simple, the language of truth
Love makes a folk song a sweet symphony
I thought it was happening,
Thought it was happening, happening to me

(Barnes Boffey and Paul Pilcher, THE VELVETEEN RABBIT,
Dramatic Publishing Co., 1974.)

What You Gotta Do

I just got off the phone with an old friend, one of two men who pulled me out of a hotel room in Pittsburgh in 1975. I was drunk and had called a hotline for help. They arrived, and after a long conversation, I was headed to a Twelve-Step meeting.

In our conversation, he related that what he had learned most from that event is that "you gotta do what you gotta do." He didn't especially want to leave home that night and talk to a drunk in a hotel room, but he had made the commitment to always be available when the cry for help was heard. He did what he had to do, and it changed our lives forever.

As we talked, I realize how grateful I am that he followed his heart and made the visit. He could never have known that his action would be so important in changing my life, but he had enough faith to just take the next step in front of him. I hope I am always there that way for others.

You just gotta do what you gotta do!

Fear Begets Fear

Fear is self-perpetuating. Every time we validate our fear by acting on it, we lose power to overcome it. Like a muscle being exercised, the fear becomes stronger each time it is used.

If we are afraid of flying and we don't get on the airplane, we will be even more fearful next time the opportunity arises. If we are afraid of telling the truth and we hold back because of that fear, we will be even more afraid of the truth in the future.

We may believe we can decrease fear by giving into it, but after a moment of relief, the fear increases. Waiting for the fear to go away because we are afraid to face it creates an ever-widening hole in our soul. We must choose faith and courage in spite of the fear.

Fear of Financial Insecurity

The fear of financial insecurity can feel like a whirlpool with no bottom. We imagine we don't have or won't have enough money, and we begin to make decisions based on that fear. Acting on fear creates more fear, and acting on scarcity creates more scarcity. When we feel financially insecure, it seems so overwhelming that we can hardly imagine that it really isn't an issue of money.

In actuality, it's an issue of spirit and attitude. If we focus on the problem as if it were financial rather than spiritual, we will never escape the whirlpool.

In times of worry about money, I have found that the best cure is to give a donation to a favorite charity or a generous gift to a friend or loved one. The amount is not important as long as it represents "a little more than I think I can afford."

Walking through the fear is affirmation that my faith and courage are stronger than my doubt and fear. Once I restore my spiritual balance, I can focus on the monetary issues with optimism and faith.

Where You Start Doesn't Matter

Sometimes we feel overwhelmed when we think about certain issues — unresolved conflict, family relationships, job problems, and all our fears, feelings, and dreams. We look at the knot of issues and don't know where to begin.

Facing all the issues in our lives is like cleaning an entire house. If the goal is to clean the whole house, where we start is just a matter of personal preference. We can start with the stove or the furniture or the dusting. The fact *that we start* is more important than *where we start*.

Taking a step into faith and action breaks the cycle of feeling overwhelmed.

Kilometers Away

Kilometers away,
   there are shells of fear and death
      landing in the lives of people I do not know.

And as I sit here and wonder about being here ...
   I think about them there, and me here,
      and them here, and me there,
   and I try to make sense of the tragedy and
      stupidity
         Without a way to make sense
            and give meaning,
this reality becomes a place of hopelessness —
   the stuff of despair.
To make sense of the senselessness and create
   meaning in the meaninglessness
      is the heart of dignity, of hope, of
         compassion.

I am not afraid to die — of that I am sure.
But to die without dignity — of that I am afraid.

To create dignity is to do what God has asked me to do and
to do it even in situations where others have
   forgotten about dignity,
      and being,
         and God,
            and others.

My GodJob is to teach the thinking of peace,
  of that I am also sure.
For with the thinking of war,
  we create war;
and with the thinking of peace,
  we create peace.

Perhaps in this room is a voice
  that will lead this country out of its sadness;
Perhaps in this room is a voice
  that will spark the light of wisdom in the
    darkness of ignorance;

Surely in this room are those who will help
  to weave the fabric of peace
    that is even now being designed in our
      hearts and minds.

When I think I need to be somewhere else
  to be of more use,
I realize
  that if I were to leave
  I would not be here to support
    that voice ...
and that would be the greatest loss of all.

I am here to be with you, for here we create
  peace, and love, and dignity;
    from here we must share the light of truth.

It can only begin with me ... it can only begin with us.

(This poem was written in Croatia during the war with Serbia in 1995.
Word had just come through to our conference that the Croatian capital,
Zagreb, was being bombed.)

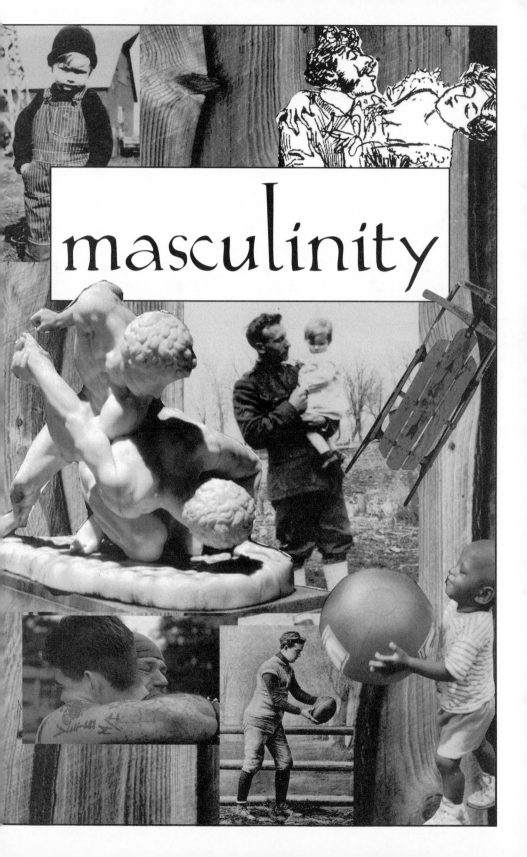

masculinity

Defining Masculinity

Men spend much of their early lives trying to live up to a single ideal of manhood — one of strength, athleticism, and take-charge leadership. They search for *the* right way to be "a man" rather than for a right way for each of them to be a man. Men don't hear early enough or loud enough that "THERE ARE MANY WAYS TO BE A MAN!" There is no one definition of manhood that works for everyone.

When my older son David was entering ninth grade and struggling with his choice between two private schools, he eventually said, "Dad, I think School A is a better school, but I think School B is a better school for me." He took a step forward in understanding that *his* life is *his* life, and the choices he makes must be made in accordance with the man he is and the man he wants to be.

To be free, men must learn to *celebrate the differences* in each other, and then teach our sons to do the same.

What Boys Want to Know

In *The Wonder of Boys*, author Michael Gurian says that boys need to know three things before they can relax and settle into a situation: Who's in charge? What are the rules? And what is the mission?

I have been working with boys for many years, and this rings true. Boys don't relax until they know that someone is running the show, and that he or she will maintain order and keep everyone safe.

They want to know what is expected of them and what they can expect of others. They have a strong sense of fairness and territory and they want to make sure both of these are preserved. The rules define the boundaries.

Finally, they want to know what they are going to be asked to do. Boys want more than just to be together; they want an action step and a goal to achieve. They want a mission to accomplish. When we clarify the purpose for action, boys bring focus to the task and feel that they are moving toward success.

(Michael Gurian, THE WONDER OF BOYS, Tarcher/Putnam Publications, 1997.)

Boys Are Boys

One of the hardest things about growing up as a boy is being treated somehow as a defective girl. Boys see that girls are calmer, more academically talented, better able to say what they think and feel, and more willing to do what they are asked. Girls are seen as good. Boys often perceive that they are seen as *less than*, rather than as *different from*.

Self-esteem is hard to build when the consistent message is one of inadequacy. Boys try several ways to rescue their self-esteem. Some try to be like girls, to use girls as the ideal. Finding this both a difficult task and one that gets them excluded from the world of boys, they give up, rebel, and get angry. Unfortunately, many times this anger is directed at the girls that they were trying to be like. Rather than a respectful celebration of differences, relationships between boys and girls become contests.

Boys need to be accepted and surrounded by men and women who celebrate their maleness, adults who will show them that being a boy is something to be proud of, something to enjoy, something very special in and of itself.

(These thoughts are echoed in Don Kindlon and Michael Thompson's RAISING CAIN: PROTECTING THE EMOTIONAL LIFE OF BOYS. Ballentine Books, 2000.)

The Power of a Woman's Approval

O ne of the most significant issues that boys and young men must face as they grow into adulthood is their desire for both connectedness with and independence from women. Men want to feel whole without the need to be validated by women, but they also feel incredibly nourished when they get approval from the women they value. When a woman gives her approval to both a man's strength and gentleness, he feels encouraged to explore and express more varied and balanced ways of being a man.

When men can't get this approval from the women in their lives, they may withdraw or act out. Disapproval may lead to shame and anger. Men often pretend to be totally self-sufficient, but a woman's approval can be an incredibly powerful force in their lives.

Without awareness of this, many women overlook opportunities to show approval openly and consistently. With this awareness, women can capitalize on the incredible power they have to help create the kind of healthy, self-assured, and balanced men that they so often desire as lovers, husbands, and fathers.

Embracing the Beast

E very once in a while I just need to growl, to bellow, to yell, to feel the sheer raw energy I can create. It's the part of me that loves the brute force in an Arnold Schwarzenegger action film and the part of me that roars "Yessssss!" when my football team scores.

I could pretend it isn't there but there's the beast in me that loves to have its moment. Yet there is the beauty in me also that is often afraid to let it out. I love the beast; it's a wonderful part of being human and of being a man. But standing 6'7" tall and weighing 260 pounds, it is also important that I find a way to express that energy appropriately.

As crazy as it seems sometimes, I can understand the excitement some people have about pro wrestling. It allows them to express the energy of the beast in a socially acceptable manner and to experience this power in ways few other places allow. It is not approved of in church, school, families, and most social settings. When we try to deny the beast, we lose something special, and we risk its coming out in scary, hurtful ways.

Fear of Touching

One of the saddest myths about boys, is that physical closeness to other boys and men is not healthy. Even with children of 4 and 5, fathers believe they must stop kissing or hugging them. Boys get the message there is something wrong with touching each other. Michael Thompson, in *Raising Cain*, says that men are too often afraid of having their masculinity unravel.

There are two very strong messages that get sent to boys. One, it's not OK to be a girl; men who are like girls are not real men. The other is it's not OK to be gay; men who like men are not real men. Dr. Thompson relates that boys in middle school endure an average of twenty-four anti-gay slurs each day. Our homophobia and fear of being feminine often stop us from loving our sons in tender and physical ways. We should never be afraid of touching and hugging the people we love. If we are to break through the myths of masculinity, words are not enough. A loving and appropriate touch says so much more.

The Power of Safety

One of the gaps in most men's basic training is awareness of the degree to which women need to feel safe in a relationship. Men assume that women should automatically feel safe, and that to focus on this issue is redundant and silly.

In a society in which men predominantly have the power, a woman needs to know she will not be hurt or taken advantage of by men who use that power arbitrarily or hurtfully. Finding ways to acknowledge that reality can significantly enhance a relationship. "I love you" is "I love you," but it may also mean, "Don't worry, you are safe."

Sexualizing Everything

O ne of the hardest parts of growing up male is subtly being taught to sexualize everything. There is a natural sexual energy that men have that is healthy and positive, but much of what it means to grow up male revolves around hyper-sexualization, and how it is woven into the filters through which men see the world.

In the beginning, it is fun to participate in these sexualized relationship rituals: to bring every conversation and interaction back to a sexual context. But as we grow older, we often find more and more difficulty in differentiating fact and fantasy in this important realm of our lives. Men learn to process encounters through many filters, but having the sexual one as a constant and predominant one can skew the entire process of healthy emotional and sexual development.

As men, much of the information that we learn about the overwhelming importance of sex is very out of balance, but we may not find that out until we have trouble maintaining fulfilling long-term relationships.

A Man Women Can Trust

Becoming a man that women can trust is not easy when so much of your life as a man is grounded in hunting and pursuing, and so many relationships with women have been subtly or not so subtly laden with sexual overtones. It's hard not to consistently use sexual innuendo as a standard form of communication. It's difficult not to give hugs that send mixed messages. It is a challenge to learn to share greetings that are honest expressions of friendship rather than connections full of confused sexual tension.

Becoming a trustworthy man means becoming a man that women can trust to not take advantage of vulnerability. It means becoming someone they can be honest with and not have to fear a unilateral shift to a sexual or intimate relationship.

For most of us, it takes significant effort to be a man that women can trust. It doesn't happen easily. After many years, I came to a point in my own life where I didn't like that I was always on the prowl. I like myself more now.

Male Myth #142

There is a myth that men are afraid to make long-term commitments, but in fact they often search for them. Men make undying commitments to friends, sports teams, and old T-shirts. They pledge allegiance willingly to ideals they believe in and to demanding codes of honor.

In relationships, men are less willing to commit when they feel their freedom will be severely limited by the unilateral expectations imposed by another person or that the relationship carries with it a set of demands that feel like a "package deal." Men want a line-item veto about the rules of a relationship.

The myth that men "just can't make a commitment" can be very harmful. It leads to blame and guilt rather than to a more positive focus on working out mutually agreeable expectations.

Men thrive on commitment. It gives meaning to their lives.

parenting

A Birth

Time brings us round again to know
the child of Man,
and sense with awe our own beginning;
And in seeing ourselves born
through the coming
of another,
we know that hope still smiles:
that dreams can still be dreamt,
and love fulfilled ...
And perceiving God's power in this moment
called birth,
we share at once with all humanity
our own essential goodness.

(Written on the occasion of the birth of my son Adam in 1976.)

Parental Vows

Most marriage ceremonies include a phrase that is actually more appropriate to our relationship with our children: "'Til death do us part."

In the process of life, we may change husbands and wives, but we will never change our children. They are indelibly part of the fabric of our being. We can't divorce them, we can't trade them in.

It's a wonderful and unique relationship, that of being a parent and child, and the learnings are amazing if we embrace the process. Our children, partly because of the fact that they will always be our children, become mirrors in which we see our reflections for all the years of our lives ... in fact, "'Til death do us part."

Each Day Upon Leaving

I don't remember the exact day, but I do remember the decision. I decided that each day when I left the house that the last words my children would hear from me were, "I love you."

There were times when "Don't forget to clean up your room," or "Tell your mother I'll call her later," or even "Get your bike out of the driveway" competed for the final statement. In those instances where the business of family arrangements and requests arose, it seemed even more important to take the extra moment to say, "I love you!"

It occurred to me that on any given day I might be killed in a car accident or other unforeseen event. If that happened, I always wanted my children to know that the last words they heard from their father were, "I love you!"

It's one decision I have never regretted.

The Family Pictures

If our parents were Democrats, we are likely to be Democrats. If our parents were not openly affectionate, then it is likely that we aren't either. For better or for worse, parents pass along their ideas, attitudes, and perceptions to their unsuspecting children.

My father was an alcoholic and he passed his alcoholic thinking onto me. I'm sure neither of us even knew it happened; it was just what I learned from my dad. I don't blame him. He was doing the best he could, and I'm sure he thought his view of the world would serve me well.

In the early years of my own parenting, I unwittingly began to pass these same family pictures on to my own children. It would have crippled another generation. The thought of being an accomplice appalled me. It took days and months and years of soul-searching and eventually recovering from my own alcoholism, but I think I finally broke the pattern. Some of the old pictures still got through, but most got torn to shreds.

Waiting for Mom to Get It

Blaming our parents for the way we are and for their not being who we needed them to be is a double-edged sword. In laying responsibility at their feet, we are unable to claim it for our own. In believing that our relationships with them can't change until they start parenting in a way that we deem acceptable, we continue to wait to be given our freedom; we wait for permission to become adults.

Freedom that is granted is not true freedom, for it can also be taken away. Emotional adulthood must be claimed with or without permission. The most profound step I ever took in becoming an adult child was deciding that I would start to be a good son even if my mother was not a good mother.

I wasn't being the son I wanted to be at the time, and I kept waiting for her to change the relationship by being a better mother. I was unconsciously waiting for permission to be the person I wanted to be. Realizing that, I began to treat her with more kindness and forgiveness. I wish I could say I took that step at 18, but in fact I was 40 years old.

Growing with Our Children

*Who of us is ready for offspring before the offspring themselves
arrive? The miracle of parenting is not that adults produce children,
but that children produce adults.*

— Peter De Vries

Children are like mirrors. We see them learn traits from us that
we like in ourselves and traits that we dislike in ourselves. Seeing
our strengths, we smile and take credit, but too often when we
see our weaknesses we get angry and want to blame the mirror.

Becoming adult parents means taking responsibility for the feelings and emotions we experience with our children, and focusing
more on our own behavior than on theirs. When we feel angry,
we stop blaming them and start asking ourselves how our own
expectations helped create the upset. As adult parents we look in
the mirror and take responsibility for what we see, and we change
it, realizing that getting too attached to our unrealistic expectations is usually the cause of our pain.

The Uneasy Lessons of Parenting

O ur children teach us many wonderful things, but they also create challenges that force us to learn lessons we may have no desire to master.

Would anyone look forward to learning how to clean up a diaper that seems to have exploded all over a baby, the bedclothes, and the walls?

Would anyone look forward to learning how to stay cheerful on a long trip in a small car with a moody, sullen, self-absorbed, adolescent?

Would anyone look forward to learning how to deal with the police when they call to say that your teenager has been caught buying beer?

Would anyone look forward to learning that we are not always the parents we thought we would be?

Would anyone look forward to learning how to deal with our child's pointed remark when our inadequacies are exposed for all to see?

Learning these lessons is one sign of a truly loving parent. Embracing their significance is another.

Roots and Wings

Children need to feel grounded. They also need to feel free. Too much grounding leads to fear of trying new things, and too much freedom leads to experimentation without discipline. It's the combination of roots and wings that help children learn to take appropriate risks.

A bird that won't fly is stuck in the nest. A bird that only flies never finds a home.

Character and Personality

Effective parents understand their role in their children's development. They are able to see what responsibilities they as parents should attend to and which tasks should be left to their children.

One helpful tool in making these decisions is taking into account differences between character and personality. Character involves the central values that help us make decisions and form a worldview. Personality involves establishing an identity.

A parent's most important role is to look beyond the personality and focus on character. Children and young adults can and will make most of the decisions about their individual paths as people; they may spend many hours refining their personality. Our job as parents is to maintain vigilance on the issues of character, the central core around which our children make healthy choices and moral decisions. We focus on the foundation of character; that foundation supports our children's personality.

The Important Stuff

We are much more successful parents when we focus our energies on what is significant and let go of what is not. The impulse to correct each detail of our children's behavior is both disrespectful and ultimately impossible.

Blue hair is not important. A "C" in algebra is not important. A burp at the dinner table is not important. A whole day watching TV is not important. Talking too long on the telephone is not important.

Hating people because their skin is a different color is important. Riding on the back of a motorcycle without a helmet is important. Getting pregnant at 16 is important. Abusing drugs and alcohol is important.

Treating all of the above as if they were equally significant only confuses our children. As a pope once said, "See everything, overlook a lot, correct a little."... and only the important stuff.

The Fearful Truth about Drugs

(PART 1)

Drugs create pleasurable feelings. Most adults don't want their children to know this. When people start using drugs, it is often carefree, fun, and stress reducing. For most people, there are few problems when they *start* using drugs, be they alcohol, marijuana, or cocaine.

The problems come when we *keep* using drugs and stop doing the work that a balanced life demands. It's easier for many adults to focus on the issue of never starting than to tell the truth and face the real issue, which is to not replace life with drugs.

Accepting that drugs are relatively pleasurable and problem free in the early stages is a truth we don't want to admit. But if we don't tell our kids the truth, they will stop listening to us. The distinction between pleasure and happiness is hard to understand at 15 years old, but maybe that's what we should teach our kids. First, of course, we have to learn it ourselves.

What Drugs Do

(PART 2)

In essence, every drug does the same thing. It helps us feel better with no effort required on our part. In real life, if we want to feel better, we need to put energy into thinking better and acting better. With drugs, the necessity of thought and action is eliminated. Is it any wonder they are so popular?

When an adolescent is angry and depressed about breaking up with his girlfriend and wants to feel better, he might either talk it through with friends, work to be forgiving, exercise to release some stress, or make amends for what he has done.

He might also focus on the good things the breakup may bring, he might question the role of fate in his life, he might think about other relationships that could be rewarding and he might get together with friends to play basketball or watch a movie.

Or he can have a few beers and feel better with no effort. At 15 years old that's a hard choice to make. And sometimes even at 50.

When Drugs Stop Making Sense

(PART 3)

There is no drug that can compete with the joy of being in the flow of the universe and mirroring God's will in the world.

There is no drug that can compete with living in the truth and knowing we have the courage and faith to face whatever comes our way.

There is no drug that can compete with the joy of overcoming fear, or sharing our innermost secrets with a trusted friend, or feeling free to speak our truth regardless of the reaction of others.

When we can accomplish the above, drugs become a poor substitute for life. If we can feel the joy of being in God's light, why would we want to settle for second best? Until we move toward more spiritual ways of being and working and schooling and relating to each other, drugs will maintain their powerful role in our society.

I wish the answer wasn't so hard, but we have already used up all our easy answers.

Touching Moments

A great deal of what we teach our children we teach them through touch — hugging, patting, nudging, and rolling around on the living room floor.

I taught my sons a great deal about being men in the times we spent wrestling and roughhousing. They learned they could hurt somebody if they weren't careful. They learned to listen for signals that someone wasn't having fun. They learned to say, "Stop, I really mean it," and to see the impact of that statement. They learned that if you keep trying you can get out of a tight squeeze. They learned that you better look around before you have fun or something might get broken. They learned that men can be both rough and gentle. They learned the power of a hug and the feeling of safety in being held in someone's arms.

I could have told them all these things, and in fact I probably did, but I think our time was better spent in those wonderful wrestling matches we had on the couch and living room floor.

Family Vacations

Vacations are time for change and rest, a time to break out of the normal routine. In our early years of parenting, we often look forward to a vacation with the family, expecting a chance to relax the way we did before we had children. The word *vacation* conjures up peace and quiet. No way!

There can be a very big difference between a vacation and a family outing. On a vacation, our time is our own, our schedule is flexible, and we can be alone or with our significant other without the conflicting demands of our children.

On the other hand, when taking a family outing (i.e., vacation with children), we are still on duty, but in a different locale. Extended opportunities to totally relax are infrequent, and we are still responsible for the care of others. We are still in the parent role, and our children still need our time and attention.

Both vacations and family outings are ways to break out of the routine, but getting expectations clear before we imagine a peaceful vacation can save a lot of aggravation for everyone.

More Yes, Less No

Developing responsibility in others, be they our children or employees or students, involves saying yes more than no. It may seem that drawing boundaries with a no would be most important, but *no* shifts the responsibility to us for the decision and the enforcement.

"The answer is *yes* if we can work out a way where we both feel good," shifts responsibility for the problem and invites others to help solve it.

"Help me figure out a way that I can say *yes* to your request," is another invitation, as is "I want to say *yes*, but we need to find a way to talk through a few issues before I can do that."

When we live in a world that says yes more often than no, we begin to look at opportunities rather than limitations. We solve problems rather than simply challenging authority.

Emotions on Top
of Emotions

Suppose our children are upset at us because we have enforced a family rule. No one enjoys having his children angry with him, but such is the way of parenting.

Suppose our children get angry, and then we get angry. And then we start the most destructive process of all, piling emotions on top of emotions.

We start to feel guilty that we are angry. "We shouldn't be mad at our kids, they just don't like the rule." Then, because we believe that guilt is an immature response, we become critical of ourselves. We know that being critical is what our parents did, and we don't want to repeat those patterns, so we now feel resentment toward our parents. With so much anger, we start to feel scared that anger is playing too big a part in our lives ... and we keep adding layer upon layer.

We can halt the process by asking a pivotal question: "My kids are angry at me right now. If I were the parent I wanted to be, how would I feel about that and what's my next step?" No more pile!

"You're Weird"

As well as being a lot of work, parenting is a lot of fun. One of the things that made it especially fun for me was my decision that when my kids got weird, I got weirder. When they made a goofy face to show their mild disapproval with something I had done as a parent, it seemed the perfect opportunity to lighten the mood by making an even goofier face. When they reproached me with an "Oh dad," it provided a wonderful chance to assume the role of a zany character and reply in a strange accent, "Yes, my son!"

When our children say, "You're weird," there is often a note of admiration as well as frustration. "You're weird" can be a compliment.

Adding fun to the parenting process, especially in time of stress and conflict, can facilitate the process of working things through. It's a shame to miss a chance to be silly in situations where humor is the most appropriate tool.

More Than Consequences

When children break reasonable rules, there is more to the process of parenting than creating and following through on consequences. Of course, we can send them to their rooms or have them take a time out or lose TV or phone privileges, but just taking things away does not solve the problem or bring relationships back into balance.

With the assistance of an understanding and caring adult, most children leap at the chance to right their wrongs and correct their mistakes. Giving them this opportunity allows them to come into balance and, through meaningful effort, regain their ability to be loving, powerful, playful, and free.

Fixing the problem becomes the consequence for having created the problem, and in doing so, children learn to worry less about blame, shame, anger, and fear and more about making things right. Adults who help us fix our mistakes help us gain and keep our self-respect.

Accepting Mistakes

Children make mistakes, lots of them. As parents, we need to decide early on how we will deal with them. If we are critical, our children will hide their mistakes and avoid sharing their lives. If we can help them with the embarrassment and difficulties involved with making mistakes, they will share their lives with us more openly.

- "Dad, I spilled hot chocolate on the couch."

- "Did you do it on purpose?"

- "No, of course not."

- "Then it was a mistake. How do we deal with mistakes in this family?"

- "We tell the truth and try to fix what we did wrong."

- "So how can I help you fix this problem and what can we do so it doesn't happen again?"

257

The Dorm Room Conversation

The impact of parents in the lives of children is without equal. And understanding that impact while making everyday decisions is what makes parenting such a profound experience.

As parents, we don't get a report card in any formal sense, but it has often occurred to me that one measure of my success would involve my children's evaluation during the inevitable late night conversations at camp, on neighborhood overnights, or in their college dorm room. The question always begins the same way: "So, what's your dad like?"

I knew what I hoped my children would say, and I tried to parent in a way that would lead to that end. I hoped they would say that I was fair and fun, and that I loved them, and that I gave them the freedom they needed to make mistakes and to learn to be good men.

If that's what they said, that would be a report card I would be proud to show to anyone.

managing, teaching, & leading

Leaders People Follow

In a leadership survey I recently read, I found some profound results. People were asked, "What do you want from your leaders?"

The four qualities that topped the list were:

- Leaders who tell the truth even when it's bad news.

- Leaders who keep their promises.

- Leaders who have fun with those they are leading.

- Leaders who believe in and practice "noble" values.

People want leaders who treat themselves and others with respect. People want leaders who are not afraid to face difficult issues and work toward elegant solutions. People want leaders who are people as well as bosses, and who have the wisdom and perspective to maintain a sense of humor.

A great thinker has powerful ideas. A great leader puts these ideas into practice and helps others to do so also.

People Thrive on Trust

People thrive on trust. Trust has a price, but the return on our investment can be huge. When people feel trusted, they raise their expectations of themselves. When people feel trusted, they want to show themselves worthy of that trust. When people feel trusted, they know it is a gift, and they feel gratitude.

People thrive on trust, but there will always be some who take advantage. There will be some who perceive the trust as an invitation to be selfish and self-serving, and there will be some who need more time to adapt to being trusted than we have to give. Courageous leaders and institutions search for ways to continue to trust, while also dealing with individual misconduct.

People thrive on trust, and although communities based on trust have their problems, the long-run difficulties encountered may be small in comparison to communities grounded in mistrust. Mistrust is based on fear, and fear eventually destroys both relationships and communities.

An Honest Answer

O ne of the things I like about myself as a leader is that I'm serious when I say to my staff and colleagues: "I'd rather have an honest answer than an easy answer."

I used to be afraid that too much honesty would prove to be overwhelming and leave me feeling unclear about what to do with the information. Now I realize that an honest answer helps me face the real problem and therefore make progress toward real solutions.

I am often surprised when I ask someone a question and his response is: "Do you really want me to tell you what I think?"

Hearing this, I am sometimes tempted to make a sarcastic comment like: "No, lie to me. I'll feel much better and more respected if you play me along." But usually I say, "Yes, I want to hear the truth." I like what saying that does to our relationship.

As leaders, we must remember that simply telling the truth is a courageous act, whether we ask that of others or of ourselves.

Resolving Leadership Dilemmas

Leadership always entails facing some dilemmas that have no obvious solutions. The reasoning that leads to one solution may be just as compelling as reasoning that leads to another.

A good leader resolves these dilemmas by perceiving the conflict as an opportunity to confirm core beliefs. Good leaders pose questions that help people look at the values they espouse and put those values into practice.

If we were a family that wanted to be more trustworthy, how would we resolve this issue?

If we were an organization that believed that reasonable risks were important for growth, what path would we choose in this situation?

If we were serious about being honest with people in issues that affect them, what would we tell our employees about what is going on?

Great leaders appreciate difficult situations as opportunities to reaffirm cherished principles and to help people feel the pride of acting with integrity.

When We're Needed

A simple but profound definition of leadership states that *good leaders are there when they are needed.*

Defining those times is the true art of managing, teaching, and parenting. Knowing when to be present and when we can take time away is a skill that will enable us to be both balanced and effective.

They That Have the Power

By definition, leaders have more power than their followers. It may be power over allocating resources, or power in decision-making, or power in providing feedback and determining advancement, or simply the power of influence. With that power comes the ability to help people and the ability to hurt people.

This is no secret to those who work under that power. And participating in relationships with leaders always entails a certain level of vulnerability.

Great leaders honor this vulnerability and accept their power with humility. They lead by inspiration, communication, and modeling. They minimize coercion and eliminate punishment.

William Shakespeare may have said it best: "They that have the power to hurt and will do none — they do rightly inherit heaven's graces."

Hurting Feelings, Hurting People

I once had a boss who made a staffing change that resulted in an employee moving to a different position. The new position involved less status and prestige, but it was clear to everyone (except perhaps the one employee) that the decision was warranted and best for the organization.

I later found out from my boss that at the time the employee had been transferred, her salary was not reduced, nor had there been any other actions taken that might typically be deemed as consequences of demotion.

My surprise was obvious. His answer was simple. "To run an effective organization," he said, "I am not in a position where I can always avoid hurting people's feelings, but I am in a position where I can try to avoid hurting people."

Hearing those words, I respected my boss even more than I had. He had a powerful vision.

(Thanks to Paul Pilcher.)

The Power to Forgive

A nother of the great joys of having a position of power and respect is being able to use that power to forgive.

Most of us grew up being punished for mistakes or believing that judging ourselves harshly was a way to prove we understood what we had done wrong. Unfortunately, most of us did not get the same intensity of training in the skills of forgiving ourselves and letting ourselves off the hooks we were so good at putting ourselves on.

I love to help people forgive themselves, to help them understand, as William Glasser often says, "that we are always doing the best we can with the information we have at the time." Teaching people to forgive themselves allows them to spend their time learning and correcting rather than judging and punishing. But most of us need someone who can teach us how to do this ourselves.

What a gift it is to be that person for others.

More Than a Job

Helping people find a connection between the work they do and their ability to be more spiritually fulfilled is the mark of a great leader. When people are able to make the connection, work becomes a quest as well as a job, and an expression of love as well as labor.

During the Apollo space program at NASA in the sixties, a process was designed to clarify job descriptions and responsibilities. A custodian was asked, "What does your job here entail?" He replied, "I am helping to put a man on the moon."

He saw the connection between his efforts and the greater good for himself and humankind; he understood his role as well as his job. He cleaned and swept and polished with an awareness that others could do their jobs better if he did his well.

I would like to have worked with that man.

Thank You, Mrs. Carol

She leapt into the center of people —
  the eye of the hurricane we call ourselves
and touched the parts of you you wanted
  to be touched.

And you were always glad to see her and
  she to see you —
and you knew she was;
    both glad — and really glad
    but also seeing —

beyond the walls which others attempted
  quickly and then turned from,
and beyond the time of now to then,
  when you both could see your dreams coming true ...
And she was a lady
  to be dealt with and embraced in conversation.

You know ... all she really did was run a boy's camp
called Lanakila:
and love children
    and smile at the morning
  and say hi when you needed it
    and laugh — but not too much ...
and all she *really* did
  was to be the kind of person I'd like
    to spend the rest of my life trying to be ...

(This poem was written in tribute to Carol Gulick Hulbert
for a memorial service in 1973.)

In Service to Others

Before campers arrive for the summer each year we gather all the counselors and share the camp's history and hear inspirational messages from the directors. Every year the director of the camp for younger girls finishes her talk with the same phrase that was passed along to her by a director who died many years ago: "You find yourself in service to others."

Those words have become part of who I am, and in my fifties I see myself more than ever as a teacher, a mentor, and someone devoted to passing along the love and knowledge that I have been freely given by those who have cared about me.

My thinking is not so much about what I can get as what I can give, and my goal in being with others has as much to do with what they will walk away with as what I will walk away with. Maybe I am finally beginning to understand what Helen Shaw was saying those many years ago. She showed me how to live those words; maybe I can do the same for others.

(Helen Shaw was the director of Camp Aloha Hive for many years. She was an inspiring and loving woman.)

Working For, Working At

Many years ago, while meeting a group of new people, we had the standard introductory conversation about where we worked and what we did professionally.

A friend of mine introduced me to the group and said that I "worked for Dartmouth College." I could feel a wrench in my gut, but it wasn't until later that I understood why and was able to tell him, "You know, Bill, I realized when you introduced me that I don't feel like I work *for* Dartmouth, I work *at* Dartmouth. I work *for* peace and truth and love and children. I just happen to do that *at* Dartmouth."

The difference was a profound one for me and still is. I hope that my life's work will be my life's work no matter *where* I do it: as a teacher, as a parent, as a dishwasher, as a writer, as a friend, as a husband, or as a consultant. I hope I work for the betterment of humankind and for the glorification of the human spirit. I don't ever worry that I might be out of work.

Shutting Out the Input

As a leader and parent, I often provide what I perceive to be totally valid feedback and information to others. Sometimes these people seem unwilling or unable to understand or even hear what I am trying to say; I just can't seem to get through to them. I have tried speaking louder, or speaking more forcefully, or simply reiterating the point over and over, but often to no avail.

"What are they, stupid?" has not turned out to be a very helpful approach, and I think I finally understand why this miscommunication occurs.

If we are afraid of what we will have to do if we hear certain information, we often make sure that information never gets heard. We believe that if we don't hear it, we will be spared the doubt, fear, and discomfort that come with the difficult choices that information may lead to.

Knowing this, I now ask myself, "If others were to really hear what I am saying, *what do they believe they would have to do*, and do they want to do that?" If my best guess is "No, they wouldn't want to do it," I can understand why the communication is being blocked. "Can you hear me now?"

If You Don't Know

Helping people learn is always complicated by this reality: "If you don't know you don't know, you think you know." (R.D. Laing) Without the knowledge that there is some information missing, we have no reason to put energy into learning. And, in fact, we may fight the very process that can help us break out of our *not knowing*.

Finding ways to break through this roadblock is the central dilemma in the art of teaching, managing, and parenting. In thinking *we know*, we may become quite arrogant and defensive about our way of seeing the world. It rarely works to just tell people they don't know; this is often seen as a put down. It also doesn't help to criticize them when they don't know. This leads to rebellion and anger, and arguing just leads to deeper entrenchment.

If *we don't know we don't know*, we need to surround ourselves with caring and patient people who understand what is at stake in admitting we don't know. These are the teachers and mentors who truly change our lives.

(R.D. Laing, KNOTS, Pantheon Books, 1970.)

Surpassing Expectations

In a little sliver of a book I once read entitled *The Science of Getting Rich*, the author spoke of getting rich in both a financial and spiritual sense.

His major piece of advice was: "We must give to every man a use value in excess of the cash value he receives, so that each transaction makes for more life."

The same holds true for increasing the chances of having a significant positive effect on others. By taking on the challenge of exceeding their expectations of both who we are and how far we will go to help and support them, we are likely to get their attention. With this heightened interest, they become teachable and eventually open to the idea of exceeding their own expectations. It is in the act of inspiring others to exceed their own expectations that we can have such a powerful impact on their lives.

The ability to help others transform their lives does not come from what we do for them — it comes from what we help them do for themselves.

(Wallace Wattles, THE SCIENCE OF GETTING RICH, Destiny Books, 1981.)

Taking Time to Till the Mindsoil

How much of our time as teachers, parents, and managers is spent trying to teach people things they see no use in learning? As my friend Lynn is fond of saying, "We continue to throw answers at the heads of people who have not yet asked the questions."

We need to take the time to pose the questions and help people open the doors so that information can enter. If we don't, we are like farmers throwing seed on the ground without preparing the soil. The soil is there, but there is very little chance it will nourish the seeds.

It takes time to till the mindsoil of our students, children, and employees, and that effort can feel like a waste of time when we can't see anything being accomplished. Great accomplishments take time, and preparation and readiness are at the heart of greatness. We can't rush learning if we want it to become knowledge.

(Thanks to Lynn Hulbert Adams.)

The Safety Curriculum

Several years ago I was visited by one of my former fourth-grade students. At twenty years old, she was still as energetic and intelligent as she had been as a child. In reminiscing about the good old days of fourth grade, she said, "You know what I remember most about your class? You used to walk around the class when we were working and put your hand on our shoulders. I always felt so safe."

I can never be sure what else she learned in my class, but I am happy she learned to feel safe. If we really want our students to learn things of value (not just the nine major export products of Argentina or the seven causes of the Civil War), we need to help them take risks. Real learning involves the risk of letting go of what we know to leave space for what we don't. If we want people to take risks, they need to feel safe. We won't take the risks to grow emotionally, spiritually, or intellectually if we have to protect ourselves all the time.

Belated thanks to those who put their hands on my shoulder; I wouldn't have made it without you.

Information Freely Given

I do a fair amount of speaking to groups, which sometimes includes return engagements. I have often worried that if I told them too much "good stuff" in my first meeting, I will have nothing significant to share on my return. When acting out of fear rather than faith, I sometimes found myself diluting the message to extend it further.

What I know now that I didn't know then is that my spiritual obligation is to honestly and willingly give to people the best information I have at the time. When I do that, I know I am serving them honorably and being the teacher I want to be.

When I give all I have, I am challenged to learn more. If I ever succumb to the fear of not fully sharing what I know because I'm afraid I can't learn more, I should stop speaking. At that point I will have little to pass on except fear.

Roles and Relationships

G ood teachers and good leaders always remember that when students enter classrooms or employees come to work, they arrive as much more than the role they are playing in that situation. Too often we see them primarily in their roles as students or employees rather than recognizing that:

- first, they are human beings,

- second, they are children or adults, and

- third, they are students or employees.

In attending only to this third dimension, we often lose connection with the most significant sources of energy and motivation. We can nurture that connection by acknowledging and appreciating the deeper dimensions of our students and employees.

This may be as simple as a respectful glance or a warm greeting, or as pronounced as team building or personal sharing. There is no right way to do it, but we can start by making an effort. Important roles become significant relationships when they are grounded in our deep connection as human beings.

Carol's Song

Songs may be sung and bells may be rung
In praise of your years of giving
Songs seem so small when we do recall
The way that we now are living
You've built tradition into our lives
And touched those of many others
Lanakila will always live on
Led on by its sons and brothers
We'll build a union
Of good and strong men
All Lanakilans.

Think of the campers you have involved
In camp and in all its beauty
Giving them honor, joy, and respect
For others, themselves, and duty
Four thousand or more have gone through the door
And many will follow after
Many Julys and Augusts will pass
When tears will be turned to laughter
We'll build a union
Of good and strong men
All Lanakilans.

Don't ever doubt that you are the one
Whose spirit's been here to guide us
Each of us here has some of your spark
To give to the world outside us
Hopefully now as things come to pass
The candles will still be burning
You'll stand beside to watch what we do
And help us continue learning
To build a union
Of good and strong men
All Lanakilans.

Songs may be sung and bells may be rung for you

(This song was written with Paul Pilcher in 1969 as a tribute
to Carol Gulick Hulbert, Director of Camp Lanakila
from 1922 to 1969.)

Courageous Teaching

It is only the most honorable and courageous of teachers and parents who humbly and willingly celebrate the fact that, at some point, they may know less than their students or children. They who were teachers must now become students; they who have had the power and prestige of superior knowledge must now accept that the roles may change.

It is also only the most honorable and courageous of students and children who will take on this challenge. To surpass those who have been our mentors and guides shows honor and respect. It shows that the gifts they have been given have been well used.

Fun and Formality

I had a faculty colleague at Dartmouth College tell me once that fun should not be seriously considered when trying to design curriculum or learning experiences. "This is an academic institution," he pronounced. I felt sorry for his students.

The line between formality and fun is a false dichotomy. Serious business can be conducted in an atmosphere where humor and levity play a part. Laughter opens up the heart and gives us perspective. Seeing the lighter side of life is testament to a deeper understanding.

A warm and funny story at a funeral can be the greatest tribute of all. A playful remark in a college class can bring students to life. Sharing laughter at a business meeting can renew and energize the group. It never made sense in school when the teacher said, "This is a time for work, not fun." I wish she'd taught me how to do both. I have finally learned how, and I know my students enjoy learning and school a lot more than I did.

Acknowledging the Spirit

I often greet passing strangers with a nod or a "hello." When my children were younger, they would constantly ask me, "Do you know that guy?" They hadn't yet learned that acknowledging the spirit in others is a way to nourish my own. Passing kindness onto others is what keeps it alive. Kindness gets stronger as it is expressed.

Trying to be kind is not always easy. Just try to get a phone operator to respond to a simple, "Hi, how are you?" They often freeze like a deer in a headlight when they hear the words, unable to imagine that anyone would care how they are.

One of the most simple and profound things I have ever learned to do is to take a few seconds to ask each clerk or postal worker or waitress or hardware store employee, "How are you?"

That's the simple part. And then I actually wait for an answer. That's what makes it profound.

The MVP

Our Wednesday night volleyball team had made it to the finals, and the competition was intense. As always, we had rotated team members so that everyone got to play, and except for one team member, everyone was at the top of his or her game.

In the middle of the second of three games, that player shared with the rest of the team, "I'm not having a good night, and I'm hurting the team. I'm going to take myself out of rotation and sit out." He was obviously sad that things weren't going well for him, but also realized that he was harming the team's welfare.

We lost the second game, but went on to win the third game and the championship. Everyone who played had done wonderfully, some playing the best they ever had. But when the time came for our awarding the Most Valuable Player trophy for the tournament, the choice was obvious. The player who had been willing to sit out so that the team could succeed was our most valuable player.

aging & maturing

Keeping the Child Alive

Staying in touch with the child inside us is not always easy in a world that demands that we *act our age*, but by maintaining a connection with the silliness, simplicity, and sensitivity of childhood, we are better parents, teachers, spouses, and friends.

Sometimes my wife will watch me make a funny face or spray water through my teeth at an unsuspecting friend. "You are nine years old," she says, but she says it with warmth and love. It's fun to play in front of her, knowing that it's OK.

To maintain a healthy connection to the child inside, one helpful distinction is the difference between childish and child-like. Being childish smacks of immaturity and self-centeredness; it is emotion uninformed by reason; it is desire uninformed by reality. Being child-like implies spontaneity, frivolity, and an openness to new experiences grounded in wonder and awe.

Today I rolled on the floor with our dog. I felt like a kid again. Maybe it's time to scrape the icing off the Oreo cookie with my two front teeth.

Life Stages

In the process of human creation and birth, we emerge from a purely spiritual state into one of flesh. When we die, we leave that flesh and become pure spirit again. There are definite stages to the journey.

The first third of our lives is very physical in nature. We learn to use our bodies; we crawl and run and play sports. As children we want to touch and smell and taste. We interact with the world primarily though our senses and our physical selves.

The second third of our lives is increasingly "in our heads." We interact with the world using our intellect. We think problems through, we gain employment for our ability to use ideas, and we gain strength through understanding.

The last third of our lives challenges the spiritual aspect of our being. We are getting ready for our transition to pure spirit. In this stage of our lives, we must learn to use the physical and mental prowess we have developed in the service of our soul.

Growing Up and Growing Older

As children, when we got too big for piggyback rides it was a real disappointment. "Oh, come on, Dad, one more time." We didn't want to hear that the game was over. To let go graciously, we had to have something else to fill the gap, something that not only replaced the rides themselves, but something that would fulfill the *function* the piggyback rides had played. Could we really find something else that would provide opportunities to be close with our parent and be fun too?

If we did, then moving beyond the piggyback stage was a smooth transition, and piggybacks became a wonderful memory. If not, we may have finished that stage of our life with more grumbles than gratitude.

Crying, Whining, and Complaining

If we can't learn to creatively replace what we lose as we progress through life, we may live our lives as criers and whiners and complainers.

As a result of a severe infection in my knee a few years ago, I can no longer safely play volleyball. I love volleyball. I was good at it, and it allowed me to be active with my friends at camp. I also coached a fair amount as I played, and volleyball allowed me the chance to mold separate players into a successfully functioning team — a group that worked better than the sum of its parts. Volleyball was not just a game; it allowed me to express parts of myself that I cherish and enjoy.

The challenge now is to find other activities that allow me to do these same things. If I don't accomplish that transition and many others, I may not be much fun to be with in five or ten years. You will likely still hear me moaning about my knee and spending a lot of time talking about the good old days ... you know what I mean: crying, whining, and complaining.

Releasing Volleyball

A s it turns out, I get as much satisfaction from being the director of our leadership team at camp as I did from playing volleyball. I get to help mold a group into a team, I get to be with my friends, I get to face the challenge of solving rapid-paced problems, and I'm good at it.

With a replacement activity created, I can allow volleyball to become a wonderful memory. I can watch happily as others play and look at the game the way I look at pictures of my children in a scrapbook. It was a wonderful time then. Although it's different now, it's still a wonderful time.

Creatively building new activities and desires that maintain the essence of then in the time of now is both a challenge and an opportunity. Without this ability, we begin to fear the future and cling to the past. We get stuck in the successes of yesterday and cripple our ability to succeed today and tomorrow. Learning to change is hard, but compared to what?

Changing Emotional Patterns

I may be a slow learner, but changing emotional patterns has not been easy for me! It took about five years each to substantially alter my relationship with fear, anger, and guilt. The desire to decrease the power of each came quite quickly, but actually gaining the experience using new behaviors took time.

The changes seemed to be focused in five-year clusters. From approximately ages 30 to 35 I worked on my anger, from 35 to 40 I worked on my guilt, and from 40 to 45 I made significant strides in overcoming fear as a major force in my life.

I don't regret the time I spent, and I'm not sure I could have done it any faster. Things that aren't easy take time ... and it's not a race.

On the Road to 60

In my twenties, I thought I knew it all, and I could generally make up in enthusiasm and bravado what I lacked in knowledge and experience.

In my thirties, I realized how little depth there was to what I had known in my twenties, and I began to understand that knowledge was more valuable than information.

In my forties, I saw how transparent the pronouncements of my twenties and thirties must have been to those who actually knew what I had only hoped to know, and I began to understand that thoughtful experience is what breathes life into knowledge.

In my fifties, I am enjoying being as competent as I pretended to be in my twenties, and I'm beginning to realize that wisdom is what I really wanted all along. I just couldn't have it until I got *right size* in my relationship with God and the universe.

In my fifties, I also enjoy rather than fear the reality that there's a lot I don't know yet. I wonder what my sixties have in store.

A Club I Want to Join

Several years ago, I met a woman who had started a club I wanted to join. She and a group of women had begun to meet on a regular basis to help each other live their lives in such a way that they would have no regrets when they were 80 years old.

Their "No Regrets At 80" club sounded like a wonderful idea. Imagine if we asked ourselves each day what choices we could make that would lead to a life free of regret? What experiences would we want to have? What relationships would we want to make right? What kind of a people would we want to be so that at 80 we would look back and not regret what we had done, or said, or been?

Last I heard, there were no dues or fees and the name wasn't copyrighted. Maybe we all could open a local chapter — even if only in our hearts.

(With thanks to Mary Farrell-Jones.)

Stewardship

One of the joys of being young is enjoying good and beautiful experiences for the first time. One of the joys of growing older is working to preserve those experiences so that future generations can enjoy the same. Stewardship takes a special kind of caring, vision, and love.

Several of the immense oak beams in one of the great halls at Oxford University were near the end of their usefulness. They had become weak and bug infested and needed to be replaced. But where in Britain were the trustees to find huge oak beams to replace them? In fact, where in the world? Was this the end of the special majesty of these incredible buildings?

Hoping for advice, the trustees went to the University forester and told him the dilemma. He smiled and said, "I've been wondering when you'd call me? You see, 300 years ago, the forester of Oxford knew this moment would come and he planted a secret stand of oaks to be fully matured, when you needed them." Stewardship takes a special kind of caring, vision, and love.

(Thanks to Tom Keefe for this story.)

The Fire in a Man

In the movie *Zorba the Greek*, Zorba says, "They say that age dulls the fire in a man. He hears death coming and he opens the door and he says, 'Come in, give me rest!' That is a pack of lies. I got enough fight in me to devour the world. So I fight."

"Growing older" is a physical process, a mental process, and an emotional process. "Aging" is a spiritual process. Just because we grow older doesn't mean we age. In fact, if we can continue to expand spiritually, we can actually grow younger, even in an older body.

As human beings, we are spirit housed in flesh. Spirit is eternal, and the more our lives are a reflection of our spiritual selves the more ageless we become. I actually know some older people who are some of the youngest people I know.

Old Doesn't Mean Dull

Too many people worry that as they grow old, they will automatically become dull, boring, and stodgy. The truth is that if they were dull and boring and stodgy when they were young, they will probably be dull and boring and stodgy when they are old. Age doesn't cause these things, it just creates a greater challenge.

We have choices as to how we want to grow old, just as we have choices about how we want to be young.

A *ripe old age* is the result of preparing the soil, planting with care, pruning when needed and supplying just the right amount of water, sun, and manure.

The manure really helps.

Metal Fatigue

Maintaining our dignity and grace as we get physically older demands an acceptance that our bodies have a life expectancy. After a certain number of years, we will simply start to experience the human equivalent of metal fatigue, the decrease of tensile strength when metal is used over and over again.

Watching our bodies change as they grow older is harder if we are confused about our essential nature. If we understand we are essentially spiritual, we won't be as concerned about the changes in our bodies. If we have too much emotional attachment to the concept of our physical selves, we are likely to struggle harder with the natural process of physical aging.

We can approach the process with wonder or approach it with fear. In either case it will happen. Our ability to release our bodies from the servitude of expectation helps us celebrate the process.

But only if we want to.

Death Is a Wake Up Call

K nowing we will die adds urgency to living. As Scott Peck says, "Death is what gives life its meaning." Whether it is a dreadful urgency or a delightful urgency is the choice we get to make.

In accepting that we will die, we gain a greater appreciation of each moment we are alive. If we deny death, we also deny the preciousness of life.

I was afraid of death myself until I answered two questions. The first was, "How do I feel about death?" The second was, "How do I want to feel about death?" I forget my answer to the first, but my answer to the second question was: "I want to be as unafraid of where I am going when I die as I am of where I came from before I was born."

In making that choice, I befriended death rather than seeing it as my enemy. Death seemed more like a loving parent sending me on a journey. "Have a wonderful trip, I'll see you when you get home."

(Scott Peck, THE ROAD LESS TRAVELED, Simon and Schuster, 1978.)

A Final Goodbye to My Friend

Dear Dick,

Since first we met, there has been so much growth and love between us: as friends, as students, as teachers, as "brothers," as colleagues and as playmates extrordinaire. One role flowed into the next and then back again as needed, partly because you were so humble, never caring what the role was as long as the job got done.

You never withheld your love from people because you knew that doing that would kill your spirit. I loved the fact that you were intelligently "selfish" enough to know that loving was good for others, but it was also your path to God and happiness.

They say there are two ways to provide light to the world. One is to be the candle and the other is to be the mirror that reflects it. You were both. Your light came into the hearts of each of us and gave us love, but you also stood as a mirror that we could look into and see our own strengths and weaknesses.

There were moments when I looked at you and didn't like what I saw. Against your model of generosity and compassion and patience, I saw reflections of my own greed and judgement and impatience. And yet you never commented negatively when I saw those sides of myself. You were always there with a big hug to let me continue my struggle and learn what I needed to learn.

My mother has been dying over the past few weeks, and I have learned that there are five steps that Hospice hopes that loved ones will go through as they separate from each other in the dying process. The first is to ask "Do you forgive me?" In our case, the question would be irrelevant because I know you never judged me.

The second is a statement, "I forgive you!" Again, this seems somewhat irrelevant because I loved every part of you and never thought you were doing anything other than the best you could. What was there to forgive?

The third step is for me to say to you, with a candor and depth that I know you can feel even though you are not here in body, "Dick, it was an honor and a joy to be your friend and colleague."

Step Four: "I love you."

And Step Five: "Goodbye."

I'll miss you, dear friend. I cherish our caring and our struggles and our jokes and our meals and our conversations and our rooming together and our learning to be better husbands and our hopes and our dreams and our differences. You made my life and the lives of others so much better, and I will always think of you as one of God's best gifts to me. Goodbye and be well.

(This letter honors Dick Pulk of Springfield, Vermont, a wonderful friend and colleague. This letter was written for his memorial service.)

When It's Time to Go

If I get to a point in my life where I am no longer able to lead what I consider to be a quality existence, whether due to illness or old age, I know I will have some difficult choices.

I don't think I want to wait for the random moment when my body gives out. Having some choice about when I die would be important to me. Otherwise, it reminds me of driving a car and simply going until the gas tank is empty. The journey ends when the gas is gone, with no connection to a significant place or time or event. That isn't how I live my life; why would I want to die like that?

I think I would rather drive that car to a beautiful vista and have a last conversation with friends and family. If I have the opportunity, I want the journey to end with choice. I want to return to pure spirit with elegance and dignity.

If I leave with an eighth of a tank of gas remaining, then so be it!

Thank You, Ruth

Strong heart, gentle being,
    seeing eyes that knew so much.
She stood in background lighting,
    providing context that others might shine and grow
and see their likeness in the mirror of her giving.

There was never any question of being what she was
not;
    she only knew one way ...
        grace, dignity, and strength.
You felt something bigger than the words you knew to
say;
    In all, "she was a lady."

Lives that touch other lives create sparks in the transition,
    and as she attracted the children and adults who
        saw her as safety,
    sparks flew in all directions,

    sparks of faith,
    sparks of acceptance,
    sparks of compassion,
    sparks of laughter.

Those sparks live in my heart today.

My childhood and adulthood were better because she
somehow forgave me my mistakes and stupidity,
focusing more on my hopes and goodness and my small
successes

She touched those she met and healed the hurt.
I know, because I had a lot of hurt.

I know God smiled the day he brought Ruth home.
I know he had a few things he wanted to talk about,
    and I'm sure he counted on a little time
    for a conversation with just the two of them

... She affected people that way.

I really look forward to seeing her again —
    in a dream, in a thought, in a memory, in a feeling.
I hope she knows how much we all loved her.

(This poem honors Ruth Buchanan, a wonderful friend and camp
personality who knew how to help little boys — and big boys —
feel safe and special.)

I Am Waiting for You

I am waiting for you
where the moon is full
where the sea is wide
where the sand is soft

(1991)

Thanks!

Adam Boffey
Al Katz
Al Reynolds
Al Shaler
Alan Crutchfield
Alan Johnson
Alan Pardy
Alan Wiecking
Alex Henzel
Allison Wiseman
Amrit Desai
Amy Gabarro
Amy Larson
Amy Nickerson
Andrew Watson
Andy Peterson
Andy Williams
Angele Marino
Ann Bourgeois
Ann Lutter
Annie Fetter
Antonia Zizak
Ariel Druch-Boffey
Arnold Vasca
Art Bourgeois
Audrey Healey
Barbara Garner
Barbara Hammel
Barbara Sullivan
Barbara Ward Kelso
Barry Minneha
Bart Craig
Ben Tilden
Betsy McCann
Betty Daniels
Betty Strand

Bill Culp
Bill Dunnack
Bill Huppuch
Bill Jarvis
Bill Powers
Bill Roffey
Bill Schreck
Bo Hall
Bob Baker
Bob Brinckerhoff
Bob Geckle
Bob Healey
Bob Holmberg
Bob Johnston
Bob Love
Bob Moore
Bob North
Bob Sullo
Bob White
Bonnie Dill
Bonnie Gamache
Bonnie Irwin
Bosiljka Lojk
Brad Bixby
Brad King
Brad Williams
Brian Berwick
Brian Bry
Brian Plumer
Brian Wiseman
Bridget Fariel
Brigid Farrell
Bruce Burk
Bruce Cooper
Bruce Kaler
Bruce Prum

Bryan Partridge
Caleb Ward
Carl Ehlert
Carlton Fitzgerald
Carol Adams
Carol Hartman
Carol Hulbert
Charlie Gottlieb
Charlie Pughe
Charlote Syer Hisey
Charlotte Sanborn
Cheryl McKinley
Chris Dorion
Chris Dye
Chris Frost
Chris Overtree
Chris Prum
Chris Spicer
Chuck Daniels
Chuck Kearney
Clara Butler
Cliff Lovering
Colby Connor
Connie Crawford
Cullis Mayfield
Cynthia Hayes
Cynthia Knowles
Dan Baker
Dan Boffey
Dan Davies
Danny Kerr
Danny Murphy
Dave Buchanan
Dave Foster
Dave Warren
Dave Rounds

Dave Yarington
David Hardy
David Horowitz
David M. Boffey
David M. Boffey
David Moran
David O'Neill
David Prum
David St. Jean
David Von Mettenheim
Dawna Markova
Debbie Daggs
Dee Billings
Del Goodwin
Diane Gossen
Diane Longabucco
Dianne Moore
Dick Allen
Dick Hendricks
Dick Lloyd
Dick Nessen
Dick Pulk
Dickens
Djurdjica Kolarec
Don Farrington
Don McIntosh
Don Williams
Dorcas Chaffee
Doug Dague
Doug Pilcher
Doug Walker
Dubravka Stijacic
Duff Tyler
Dwight Allen
Ed Hahn
Ed Linder
Ed McLaughlin
Ed Olander
Edo Olander
Eileen Burk
Eleanor Pilcher
Elizabeth
Elizabeth Carr
Elizabeth Gay

Ellen Bagley
Ellen Falk
Ellen Festner
Ellie Shaw
Emmy Bean
Eric Hall
Erie Volkert
Erik Semmelhack
Estelle Moore
Ev Weygant
Eva Smith
Eve Carey
Faith Dunne
Fitz-George Peters
Flo Olander
Fontaine Syer
Forrest Bartlett
Frank Eames
Frank Sladen
Frank Smallwood
Fraser Randolph
Fred Boffey
Fred Good
Fred Guggenheim
Fred Olander
Furman Walls
Gail Richardson
Gary Margolis
Gary Mitchell
Ged Swinton
Geoffrey Olander
George Nuffer
George Richardson
Germain Van Hee
Gerry Attuell
Gerry Weinstein
Gert Jones
Ginny Sullivan
Glenn Smith
Gus Wedell
Guy Modica
Harley Washburn
Harvey Harkness
Heidi Dahlberg

Heidi Haghighi
Helen Rankin Butler
Helen Shaw
Helen Swetland
Hendrick Gideonse
Herbie Hart
Herrick Jackson
Holly Glick
Holly Mayer
Holly Turner
Honey
Horace Reed
Iola Mayfield
Jac Read
Jack Koch
Jackson Boffey
Jagoda Tonsic Krema
Jake Gossen
Jan Chapman
Jan Frayling
Jan Larson
Jane Boffey
Jane Bullowa
Jane Merrill
Jane Standard Holden
Jane Williams
Janet Hall
Janet MacRae
Janet Thatcher
Jeannie Herbst
Jed Williamson
Jeff Bender
Jeff Burkuvitz
Jeff Grumley
Jeff Kahn
Jeff Plumer
Jeff Spiegel
Jennifer Mandelson
Jennifer Pilcher
Jeremy Cutler
Jill St. Coeur
Jim Fitzpatrick
Jim Hancock
Jim Hoogstad

Jim Thomas
Jo Ann Silverstein
Joan Hoogstad
Joan Larson
Joan Marchetti
Joan Prum
Joani Awahsos
John Carey
John Coffin
John Cottrell
John Davies
John Foster
John Frymoyer
John Hall
John Lavigne
John Nimock
John Purcell
John Rutherfoord
John Valby
John Van Allsburg
Jon Berger
Josipa Basic
Judy Downing
Judy Hatswell
Judy McFadden
Judy Pierpont
Julia Berwick
Julia Phelps
Julie Bucklin
Julie Johnson
June Rummler
Karen Olander
Kari Heistad
Karl Lindholm
Kate Merritt
Kate Schaefer
Kathy Christie
Kathy Dellapenna
Kathy Kiernan
Katie Pilcher
Kato Guggenheim
Kay King
Keith Keeler
Keith Witty

Kelly Lojk
Kelly Smith
Ken Carpenter
Ken Freeston
Ken Olsen
Ken Tibbets
Kenny Logan
Kerrie Morrison
Kevin Comeau
Kevin Purcell
Kim Overtree
Kt Hoffman
Lanny Springs
Larry Ashby
Larry Karp
Larry Kurdeka
Larry Larson
Larry Wrenn
Laura Attuell
Laurie Gausvik
Lee Boffey
Leon Lojk
Leslie Rower
Lewis Pilcher
Linda Kent
Linda Morgan Patchett
Linda Valley
Lindora Cabral
Lisa Taylor
Loretta Murphy
Lorraine Bixby
Lou Gardner
Louise Richardson
Lucia Williams
Lyn Haas
Lyn Woodbury
Lynn Hulbert Adams
"Ma" Foley
Maggie McGuire
Marge Hooker
Marge Scott
Marian Boultbee Brown
Marilyn Baldwin
Marilyn Leonard

Marilyn Rollings
Mark Brooks
Mark Dorion
Mark Kelso
Mark Weigel
Martha Danziger
Martha King
Martha Rich
Marti Yarington
Mary Berwick
Mary Boffey
Mary Ellen Azem
Mary Farrell-Jones
Mary Hulbert
Mary Powell
Mary Rutherford
Mary Williams
Masha Rudman
Matt Bender
Matt Gregoire
Max Utsler
Mercer Boffey
Merrill Noble
Michael Cassar
Michael Lichtenstein
Michelle Boffey
Mike McConnell
Milt Bassett
Milt Frye
"Moose" Provancha
Mrs. Voris
Nan Frymoyer
Nancy Boffey
Nancy Buck
Nancy Hayden
Nancy Pennell
Naomi Glasser
Ned Hughes
Ned Modica
Ned White
Nellie Oakes
"Nick" Nickerson
Nissa Sorenson
Ophira Druch

Pat Button
Pat O'Flaherty
Patricia Carsten
Patricia Latimer
Patti Sebestyen
Patty Michaelson
Paul Cubeta
Paul Curran
Paul Munn
Paul Oakes
Paul Pilcher
Paul Sawyer
Peg Taylor
Percy Ballantine
Perry Allison
Perry Good
Peter Boffey
Peter Christie
Peter Feldman
Peter Fitzgibbons
Peter Foley
Peter Gardner
Peter Hoover
Peter Lacey
Peter Spicer
Phil Ameden
Phil Simmineau
Phillips Stevens
Phyllis Shea
Pieter Kors
Polly McLaughlin
Posie Taylor
Preston Randall
Pril Hall
Ralph Drew
Ray Coffin Jr.
Reeve Williams
Rhea McKay
Rich Pounder
Rich Spicer

Richard Liebert
Rick Foster
Rick Frey
Rick Kuckartz
Rick Thieler
Rob Bucklin
Robb Rogers
Robert North
Robin Ward
Robin Williams
Rogers Elliott
Ron Gausvik
Ron Hawthorne
Rowe Williams
Roy Carr
Roy Lutter
Roy Whalen
Rudy Glocker
Russ Leonard
Ruth Buchanan
Ruth Read
Sali Azem
Sally Lock
Sam Mercer
Sam Silverstein
Sandy Spicer
Sandy White
Sarah Littlefield
Sayre Merritt
Scott McFadden
Scott Vickers
Scott Sperry
Sharon Boffey
Sharon Peterson
Shel Ball
Shelley Brierley
Shelley Roy
Shilene Noe
Sid Simon
Sidney Jarvis

Simon Holdaway
Skip Brown
Sofian McAlary
Steve Allison
Steve Hall
Steve Langsdorf
Steve Nelson
Steve Payne
Steve Risberg
Sunshine
Susan Morgan
Suzy Hallock
Sylvia Tucker
Tavian Mayer
Ted Mitchell
Teri Lamb Motley
Erlenge "Tex" Strand
Tim Bucklin
Tim Nashua
Tim Rummell
Tommy Dickie
Tom Keefe
Tom Parrott
Trin Sandeen
Valerie Pilcher
Virginia Berwick
Wade Breed
Walter Love
Walter Rogers
Wendall Walker
Wendy Davies
Will Boehne
William Glasser
Win Ameden
Winky Stearns Hussey
Wybie Mercer
Zach Bouchard
Zach Cutler

. . . and many, many more!

About the Author

Dr. Barnes Boffey is currently the director of Camp Lanakila in Fairlee, Vermont, as well as director of Success Counseling for the Aloha Foundation. Over the years he has been an auto mechanic, a fourth-grade teacher, a professional football player, a college professor, the director of teacher preparation at Dartmouth College, a management consultant, a therapist in private practice, a senior instructor in organizations teaching Choice Theory, Control Theory, and Reality Therapy, as well as a father, husband, ex-husband and recovering alcoholic.

Barnes has helped thousands of participants move closer to becoming the people they want to be through his workshops and seminars in England, Australia, Canada, Slovenia, Croatia, and throughout the United States.

His writings include poetry, co-authoring a musical version of "The Velveteen Rabbit," and numerous articles on Success Counseling, Effective Discipline, Being a Life Changer, and Creating Healthy Communities. Barnes is also the author of *Reinventing Yourself: A Control Theory Approach to Becoming the Person You Want to Be*.

He can be reached at MyGiftinReturn@hotmail.com